Mountain Biking
Northern
New England

Dennis Coello's America by Mountain Bike Series

Mountain Biking
Northern
New England

*Dennis Coello's America by
Mountain Bike Series*

*Maine
New Hampshire
Vermont*

Paul Angiolillo

Foreword, Introduction, and Afterword
by Dennis Coello, Series Editor

Formerly *The Mountain Biker's Guide
to Northern New England*

Menasha
Ridge Press

FALCON™

Photos by the author unless otherwise credited
Maps by Tim Krasnansky
Cover photo: On the trail in Putney, Vermont, by Brooks Dodge

Menasha Ridge Press
3169 Cahaba Heights Road
Birmingham, Alabama 35243

Falcon Press
P.O. 1718
Helena, Montana 59624

♻ Text pages printed on recycled paper

CAUTION

Outdoor recreation activities are by their very nature potentially hazardous. All participants in such activities must assume the responsibility for their own actions and safety. The information contained in this guidebook cannot replace sound judgement and good decision-making skills, which help to reduce risk exposure, nor does the scope of this book allow for disclosure of all the potential hazards and risks involved in such activities.

Learn as much as possible about the outdoor recreation activities you participate in, prepare for the unexpected, and be safe and cautious. The reward will be a safer and more enjoyable experience.

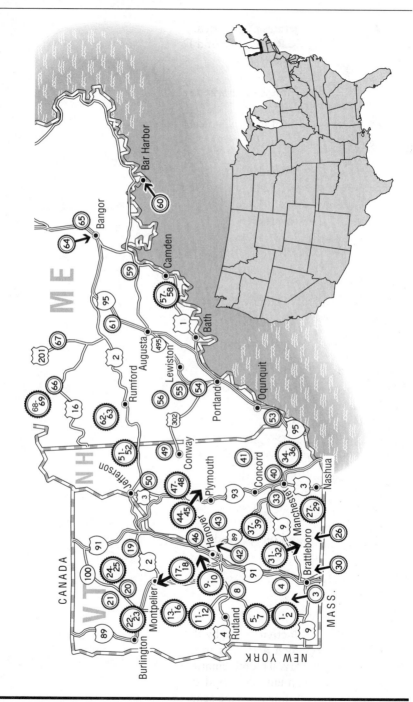

Table of Contents

AMERICA BY MOUNTAIN BIKE *MAP LEGEND*

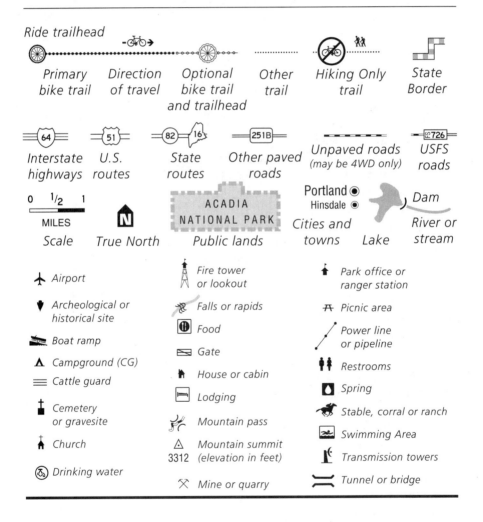

Ride trailhead

Primary bike trail   **Direction of travel**   **Optional bike trail and trailhead**   **Other trail**   **Hiking Only trail**   **State Border**

Interstate highways   **U.S. routes**   **State routes**   **Other paved roads**   **Unpaved roads** (may be 4WD only)   **USFS roads**

Scale   **True North**   **Public lands** (ACADIA NATIONAL PARK)   **Cities and towns** (Portland, Hinsdale)   **Lake**   **River or stream**   **Dam**

✈ Airport

♥ Archeological or historical site

🚤 Boat ramp

▲ Campground (CG)

═ Cattle guard

† Cemetery or gravesite

♠ Church

♿ Drinking water

🗼 Fire tower or lookout

🌊 Falls or rapids

🅘 Food

▱ Gate

♦ House or cabin

▭ Lodging

♨ Mountain pass

△ Mountain summit
3312 (elevation in feet)

✕ Mine or quarry

♠ Park office or ranger station

⇮ Picnic area

╱ Power line or pipeline

👫 Restrooms

♦ Spring

🐎 Stable, corral or ranch

🏊 Swimming Area

⌇ Transmission towers

⌣ Tunnel or bridge

List of Maps

Foreword

Welcome to *America by Mountain Bike,* a twenty-book series designed to provide all-terrain bikers with the information necessary to find and ride the very best trails everywhere in the mainland United States. Whether you're new to the sport and don't know where to pedal, or an experienced mountain biker who wants to learn the classic trails in another region, this series is for you. Drop a few bucks for the book, spend an hour with the detailed maps and route descriptions, and you're prepared for the finest in off-road cycling.

My role as editor of this series was simple: First, find a mountain biker who knows the area and loves to ride. Second, ask that person to spend a year researching the most popular and very best rides around. And third, have that rider describe each trail in terms of difficulty, scenery, condition, elevation change, and all other categories of information that are important to trail riders. "Pretend you've just completed a ride and met up with fellow mountain bikers at the trailhead," I told each author. "Imagine their questions, be clear in your answers."

As I said, the *editorial* process—that of sending out riders and reading the submitted chapters—is a snap. But the work involved in finding, riding, and writing about each trail is enormous. In some instances, our authors' tasks are made easier by the information contributed by local bike shops or cycling clubs, or even by the writers of local "where-to" guides. Credit for these contributions is provided in each chapter, and our sincere thanks go to all who have helped.

But the overwhelming majority of trails are discovered and pedaled by our authors themselves, then compared with dozens of other routes to determine if they qualify as "classic"—that area's best in scenery and cycling fun. If you've ever had the experience of pioneering a route from outdated topographic maps, or entering a bike shop to request information from local riders who would much prefer to keep their favorite trails secret, or know how it is to double- and triple-check data to be positive your trail info is correct, then you have an idea how each of our authors has labored to bring about these books. You and I, and all the mountain bikers of America, are the richer for their efforts.

Dennis Coello
Salt Lake City

P.S. You'll get more out of this book if you take a moment to read the next few pages explaining the "Trail Description Outline." Newcomers to mountain biking might want to spend a minute, as well, with the Glossary, so that terms like *hardpack, single-track,* and *windfall* won't throw you when you come across them in the text. "Topographic Maps" will help you understand a biker's need for topos and tell you where to find them. And the section titled "Land-Use Controversy" might help us all enjoy the trails a little more. Finally, though this is a "where-to," not a "how-to" guide, those of you who have not traveled the backcountry might find "Hitting the Trail" of particular value. All the best.

Preface

by *Paul Angiolillo*

Riding a mountain bike in northern New England is like being a kid in a candy store. It's hard to choose from all the possibilities—secluded trails in the grand White Mountains of New Hampshire, pastoral rides through the Green Mountains of Vermont, panoramic loops along the seacoast in Maine's Acadia National Park, hundreds of miles of dirt roads and ski trails—and more. Add four distinct seasons, which transform the riding conditions and scenery, and you've got an awesome diversity.

Collecting these rides was a lot of fun. I visited local bike shops, studied all kinds of maps, and rode with many local mountain biking gurus. I tackled hundreds of trails and was captivated by Vermont's Northeast Kingdom, known for its unspoiled beauty, Maine's rugged seacoast, and the extensive trails in the many state forests and parks.

Some of the rides are easy to follow. Others link up several routes, including two-wheel-drive dirt roads, rugged four-wheel-drive roads, and trails. It was a challenge to describe some of these longer and more elaborate rides, and following them will be easier if you have a detailed map and compass with you on the trail.

Furthermore no book (or map) can take into account all the vagaries and complexities of Nature. Things change. A storm fells a tree. A beaver dams a pond. A human cuts a new road. I've described these routes as they were when I pedaled them. But you'll be wise to keep a lookout for alterations in the landscape.

My ultimate hope is that these rides will entice more people to explore scenic unpaved roads, forgotten byways, and little-used trails on their mountain bikes. It's a great way to enjoy natural beauty, historical sites, and quiet New England villages—and have a rollicking good time!

While cruising through places like Putney, Vermont, Jackson, New Hampshire, or Hope, Maine, you don't want to be labeled a "flatlander"—a city slicker, a greenhorn, someone from a place like Boston. To avoid that ignominious fate it helps to know a fact or two about the weather, history, riding policies, bike shops in the region, and what kinds of maps you'll need.

Weather. With its warm days, cool nights, and radiant colors, autumn is the favorite time for being outside in New England. The landscape of brilliant maples, oaks, ashes, and other deciduous trees attract thousands of "leaf peeping" tourists each September and October. Whether you're riding deep in the woods or high on a ridge, autumn in this region will amaze you.

More and more mountain bikers in northern New England ride in the winter, too, using hundreds of miles of trails that become frozen and packed down by snowmobilers. This is the time to enjoy open views and absolute stillness. And

Mountain biking as a water sport.

after an invigorating ride on a crusty trail, warm up with a cup of hot chowder or cider.

Early spring in northern New England is mud season. While some riders, known locally as "mud puppies," enjoy riding through primordial ooze, others prefer to wait until the ground becomes more solid in April or May.

In late spring and summer, mosquitoes can be a bother in some areas, especially the wetter ones. If you're sensitive to biting bugs, carry an insect repellent. In my experience, though, one is usually traveling faster than bugs can fly. And the inspiring lakes, streams, and shady trails in New England in the summer far outweigh the nuisance of an insistent insect or two.

History. Sometimes it's impossible to take in your surroundings, for instance, when descending on a rocky trail while maneuvering around large boulders and catching air over smaller ones. At times like that you're wired into the trail. On less technical stretches, however, try absorbing some of the half-hidden history along the byways in this once thickly settled region. Look for old cellar holes, abandoned orchards, and the remains of mills and quarries. My favorite sites are old cemeteries, where early settlers now rest, having left behind miles and miles of impressive stone walls.

Riding Policies. Later in the book, I discuss mountain biking policies in local national forests. Vermont is generally the most sensitive of the three states to any possible environmental abuse. Rugged New Hampshire has a more lenient attitude toward mountain biking; for the most part, if you ride some of their rockier trails you'll receive only their respect. Maine is sparsely populated and thus has had few trail-user conflicts. As always, though, the most important "policy" is for cyclists to be considerate, friendly, and if necessary, to explain to the curious what mountain biking is—and is not—all about. Also, if you happen to live near a trail, you might consider "adopting" it by helping a local conservation group or park manager maintain it.

Bike Shops. For equipment, repairs, and local trail information, drop into a local bike shop; many in New England now specialize in mountain biking. These meccas for "hammerheads" often display topographical maps with rides highlighted, and act as meeting places for group rides. I've listed such shops whenever they're near a ride.

Maps. As mentioned above, for some rides you will want a more detailed map than those present in this book. Trail maps are often available at a bike shop, a park headquarters, or at outdoor equipment stores. You might also consider purchasing one of the three gazetteers published for this region (one for each state) by the DeLorme Mapping Company, Box 298, Freeport, ME, 04032, (207) 865-4171. They are also available in many outdoor and tourist-oriented stores. These large (11" × 15") books of maps show all the roads, byways, jeep trails, and once-existing routes.

Finally, United States Geological Survey (USGS) maps (called "topo" maps) are valuable because they show the topography—the ups and downs—of an area. Be sure to check the revision date on a USGS map, however; if the map was last revised in 1978, for instance, it will not show the new roads or trails created since then. With few exceptions, all the USGS maps cited in this book are the 7.5 minute series (1:25,000 scale), which means they cover an area equivalent to 7.5 degrees of latitude and longitude. In a few cases, where indicated, the USGS map available is the older 15 minute version.

A few thanks are in order. My patron was Bill Darby, who now builds custom human-powered vehicles in Cambridge, Massachusetts. He provided me with a bike, parts, accessories, and clothing.

I am also grateful to the Globe Corner Bookstore (Boston and Cambridge, Massachusetts) for donating many maps and reference books.

Finally, this book owes its existence to several dozen mountain bikers and their supporters throughout northern New England—half of whose names I unfortunately left in a notebook in Bar Harbor, Maine. Without their help I would probably still be wandering around in the woods.

James McDonough	Thomas Yennerell
Rob McDonald	Doon Hinderyckx
Dave King	Howard Stone
John Briggs	Martin Frank
Steve St. Martin	Mike Micucci

Lauren Hefferon
Fred McLaughlin
Mike Walsh
Paul Fisher
Neil Quinn
Richard Caplan
Paul Mikalauskas
Erik, Stan, and John
Ted Wojcik
Rick Frederick
Dave Larkin
Susan Cochran
Rob Roy Macgregor
Bruce Harrington
Warren Kitzmiller
John Hibshman
Abi Spring
Bob Patterson
Michael Saras
Malcolm McNair
Irv Gross
Vikki Budasi
Barbara Morris

William Laffer
Tom Mowatt
Joe Sloane
Dave Cochran
Peter Munich
Barbara Ciesliski
Duncan Thorne
Curtis Jackson
Stu Fraizer
Helena Sullivan
Raymond Dow
Steven Wilson
John Rankin
Bill Spenser
Chris Graupe
Greg, Brian, and Greg
Jamie Huntsman
Thad Dwyer
Chuck Simpson
Linda Abrahms
Jason Tillinghast
Skip Carlson

Introduction

Information on each trail in this book begins with a general description which includes length, configuration, scenery, highlights, trail conditions, and difficulty. Additional description is contained in eleven individual categories. The following will help you to understand all of the information provided.

Trail name: Trail names are as designated on USGS (United States Geological Survey) or Forest Service or other maps, and/or by local custom.

Length: The overall length of a trail is described in miles, unless stated otherwise.

Configuration: This is a description of the shape of each trail—whether the trail is a loop, out-and-back (that is, along the same route), figure-eight, trapezoid, isosceles triangle . . . , or if it connects with another trail described in the book.

Difficulty: This provides, at a glance, a description of the degree of physical exertion required to complete the ride and the technical skill required to pedal it. Authors were asked to keep in mind the fact that all riders are not equal, and thus to gauge the trail in terms of how the middle-of-the-road rider—someone between the newcomer and Ned Overend—could handle the route. Comments about the trail's length, condition, and elevation change will also assist you in determining the difficulty of any trail relative to your own abilities.

Condition: Trails are described in terms of being paved, unpaved, sandy, hard-packed, washboarded, two- or four-wheel-drive, single-track or double-track. All terms that might be unfamiliar to the first-time mountain biker are defined in the Glossary.

Scenery: Here you will find a general description of the natural surroundings during the seasons most riders pedal the trail and a suggestion of what natural occurrences can be found at certain times, such as great fall foliage or cactus in bloom.

Highlights: Towns, major water crossings, historical sites, etc., are listed.

General location: This category describes where the trail is located in reference to a nearby town or other landmark.

Elevation change: Unless stated otherwise, the figure provided is the total gain and loss of elevation along the trail. In regions where the elevation variation is not extreme, the route is described in a more general manner of flat, rolling, or as possessing short steep climbs or descents.

Season: This is the best time of year to pedal the route, taking into account trail condition (for example, when it will not be muddy), riding comfort (when the weather is too hot, cold, or wet), and local hunting seasons.

Note: Because the exact opening and closing dates of deer, elk, moose, and antelope seasons often change from year to year, it is suggested that riders check with the local Fish and Game department, or call a sporting goods store (or any place that sells hunting licenses) in a nearby town. Wear bright clothes in fall, and don't wear suede jackets while in the saddle. Hunter's-orange tape on the helmet is also a good idea.

Services: This category is of primary importance in guides for paved-road tourers, but is far less crucial to most mountain bike trail descriptions because there are usually no services whatsoever to be found. Authors have noted when water is available on desert or long mountain routes, and have listed the availability of food, lodging, campgrounds, and bike shops. If all these services are present, you will find only the words "All services available in. . . ."

Hazards: Special hazards like steep cliffs, great amounts of deadfall, or barbed-wire fences very close to the trail are noted here.

Rescue index: Determining how far one is from help on any particular trail can be difficult due to the backcountry nature of most mountain bike rides. Authors therefore state the proximity of homes or Forest Service outposts, nearby roads where one might hitch a ride, or the likelihood of other bikers being encountered on the trail. Phone numbers of local sheriff departments or hospitals have not been provided because, again, phones are almost never available. Besides, if a phone is reached the local operator will connect you with emergency services.

Land status: This category provides information regarding whether the trail crosses land operated by the Forest Service, Bureau of Land Management, a city, state, or national park, whether it crosses private land whose owner (at the time the author did the research) allowed mountain bikers right of passage, and so on.

Note: Authors have been extremely careful to offer only those routes that are open to bikers and are legal to ride. However, because land ownership changes over time, and because the land-use controversy created by mountain bikes still has not subsided totally, it is the duty of each cyclist to look for and to heed signs warning against trail use. Don't expect this book to get you off the hook when you're facing some small-town judge for pedaling past a "Biking Prohibited" sign erected the day before. Look for these signs, read them, and heed the advice. And remember, there's always another trail.

Maps: The maps in this book have been produced with great care, and in conjunction with the trail-following suggestions, will help you stay on course. But as every experienced mountain biker knows, things can get tricky in the backcountry. It is therefore strongly suggested that you avail yourself of the detailed information found in the 7.5 minute series USGS (United States Geological Survey) topographic maps. In some cases, authors have found that specific Forest Service or other maps may be more useful than the USGS quads, and tell how to obtain them.

Finding the trail: Detailed information on how to reach the trailhead and where to park your car is provided here.

Sources of additional information: Here you will find the address and/or phone number of a bike shop, governmental agency, or other source from which trail information can be obtained.

Notes on the trail: This is where you are guided carefully through any portions of the trail that are particularly difficult to follow. The author also may add information about the route that does not fit easily into the other categories.

ABBREVIATIONS

The following road-designation abbreviations are used in the *America by Mountain Bike* series:

CR	County Road
FR	Farm Route
FS	Forest Service road
I-	Interstate
IR	Indian Route
US	United States highway

State highways are designated with the appropriate two-letter state abbreviation, followed by the road number. *Example:* UT 6 = Utah State Highway 6.

Postal Service two-letter state code

AL	Alabama		LA	Louisiana
AK	Alaska		ME	Maine
AZ	Arizona		MD	Maryland
AR	Arkansas		MA	Massachusetts
CA	California		MI	Michigan
CO	Colorado		MN	Minnesota
CT	Connecticut		MS	Mississippi
DE	Delaware		MO	Missouri
DC	District of Columbia		MT	Montana
FL	Florida		NE	Nebraska
GA	Georgia		NV	Nevada
HI	Hawaii		NH	New Hampshire
ID	Idaho		NJ	New Jersey
IL	Illinois		NM	New Mexico
IN	Indiana		NY	New York
IA	Iowa		NC	North Carolina
KS	Kansas		ND	North Dakota
KY	Kentucky		OH	Ohio

OK	Oklahoma	UT	Utah
OR	Oregon	VT	Vermont
PA	Pennsylvania	VA	Virginia
RI	Rhode Island	WA	Washington
SC	South Carolina	WV	West Virginia
SD	South Dakota	WI	Wisconsin
TN	Tennessee	WY	Wyoming
TX	Texas		

TOPOGRAPHIC MAPS

The maps in this book, when used in conjunction with the route directions present in each chapter, will in most instances be sufficient to get you to the trail and keep you on it. However, these maps cannot begin to provide the detailed information found in the 7.5 minute series USGS (United States Geological Survey) topographic maps. Recognizing how indispensable these are to bikers and hikers alike, many bike shops and sporting goods stores now carry topos of the local area.

But if you're brand new to mountain biking you might be wondering, "What's a topographic map?" In short, these differ from standard "flat" maps because they indicate not only linear distance, but elevation as well. One glance at a topo will show you the difference, for "contour lines" are spread across the map like dozens of intricate spider webs. Each contour line represents a particular elevation, and each topo has written at its base a particular "contour interval" designation. Yes, it sounds confusing if you're new to the lingo, but it truly is a simple and wonderfully helpful system. Keep reading.

Let's assume that the 7.5 minute series topo before us says "Contour Interval 40 feet," and that the short trail we'll be pedaling is two inches in length on the map and crosses five contour lines between its beginning and end. What do we know? Well, because the linear scale of this series is two thousand feet to the inch (roughly 2¾ inches representing a mile), we know our trail is approximately four-fifths of a mile long (2″ × 2,000′). But we also know we'll be climbing or descending two hundred vertical feet (5 contour lines × 40 feet each) over that distance. And the elevation designations written on occasional contour lines will tell us if we're heading up or down.

The authors of this series warn their readers of upcoming terrain, but only a detailed topo gives you the information that enables you to pinpoint your position exactly on a map, steer you toward optional trails and roads nearby, plus let you know at a glance if you'll be pedaling hard to take them. It's a lot of information for a very low cost. In fact, the only drawback with topos is their size— several feet square. I've tried rolling them into tubes, folding them carefully, even

One of New Hampshire's main crops: big rocks.

cutting them into blocks and photocopying the pieces. Any of these systems is a pain, but no matter how you pack the maps you'll be happy they're along.

Major universities and some public libraries also carry topos; you might try photocopying the ones you need to avoid the cost of buying them. But if you want your own and can't find them locally, write to:

USGS Map Sales
Box 25286
Denver, CO 80225

Ask for an index while you're at it, plus a price list and a copy of the booklet *Topographic Maps*. In minutes you'll be reading them like a pro.

A second excellent series of maps available to mountain bikers is that put out by the United States Forest Service. If your trail runs through an area designated as a national forest, look in the phone book (white pages) under the United States Government listings, find the Department of Agriculture heading, and then run your finger through that section until you find the Forest Service. Give them a call and they'll provide the address of the regional Forest Service office, from which you can obtain the appropriate map.

LAND-USE CONTROVERSY

A few years ago I wrote a long piece on this issue for *Sierra Magazine* and called literally dozens of government land managers, game wardens, mountain bikers, and local officials, to get a feeling for how ATBs were being welcomed on the trails. All that I've seen personally since, and heard from my authors, indicates there hasn't been much change. Which means we're still considered the new kid on the block, that we have less right to the trails than horses and hikers, and that we're excluded from many areas including:

a) wilderness areas
b) national parks (except on roads and those paths specifically marked "bike path")
c) national monuments (except on roads open to the public)
d) most state parks and monuments (except on roads and those paths specifically marked "bike path")
e) an increasing number of urban and county parks, especially in California (except on roads and those areas specifically marked "bike path")

Frankly, I have little difficulty with these exclusions and would, in fact, restrict our presence from some trails I've ridden (one time) due to the environmental damage and chance of blind-siding the many walkers and hikers I met up with along the way. But these are my personal views. They should not be interpreted as those of the authors and are mentioned here only as a way to introduce the land-use problem and the varying positions on it, which even mountain bikers hold.

You can do your part in keeping us from being excluded from even more trails by riding responsibly. Many local and national off-road bicycle organizations have been formed with exactly this in mind, and one of the largest—NORBA, the National Off-Road Bicycle Association—offers the following code of behavior for mountain bikers:

1. I will yield the right-of-way to other non-motorized recreationists. I realize that people judge all cyclists by my actions.
2. I will slow down and use caution when approaching or overtaking another cyclist and will make my presence known well in advance.
3. I will maintain control of my speed at all times and will approach turns in anticipation of someone around the bend.
4. I will stay on designated trails to avoid trampling native vegetation, and I will minimize potential erosion of trails by not using muddy trails or short-cutting switchbacks.
5. I will not disturb wildlife or livestock.
6. I will not litter. I will pack out what I pack in, and pack out more than my share whenever possible.

7. I will respect public and private property, including trail use signs, no trespassing signs, and I will leave gates as I have found them.
8. I will always be self-sufficient and my destination and travel speed will be determined by my ability, my equipment, the terrain, the present and potential weather conditions.
9. I will not travel solo when bikepacking in remote areas. I will leave word of my destination and when I plan to return.
10. I will observe the practice of minimum impact bicycling by "taking only pictures and memories and leaving only waffle prints."
11. I will always wear a helmet whenever I ride.

Now, I have a problem with some of these—number nine, for instance. The most enjoyable mountain biking I've ever done has been solo. And as for leaving word of destination and time of return, I've enjoyed living in such a way as to say, "I'm off to pedal Colorado. See you in the fall." Of course it's senseless to take needless risks, and I plan a ride and pack my gear with this in mind. But for me, number nine smacks too much of the "never-out-of-touch" mentality. And getting away from civilization, deep into the wilds, is, for many people, what mountain biking's all about.

All in all, however, theirs is a good list, and surely we mountain bikers would be liked more, and excluded less, if we followed the suggestions. But let me offer a "code of ethics" I much prefer, one given to cyclists by Utah's Wasatch-Cache National Forest office.

Study a Forest Map Before You Ride
Currently, bicycles are permitted on roads and developed trails within the Wasatch-Cache National Forest except in designated Wilderness. If your route crosses private land, it is your responsibility to obtain right-of-way permission from the landowner.

Keep Groups Small
Riding in large groups degrades the outdoor experience for others, can disturb wildlife and usually leads to greater resource damage.

Avoid Riding on Wet Trails
Bicycle tires leave ruts in wet trails. These ruts concentrate runoff and accelerate erosion. Postponing a ride when the trails are wet will preserve the trails for future use.

Stay on Roads and Trails
Riding cross-country destroys vegetation and damages the soil.

Always Yield to Others
Trails are shared by hikers, horses and bicycles. Move off the trail to allow horses to pass and stop to allow hikers adequate room to share the trail. Simply yelling "Bicycle!" is not acceptable.

Control Your Speed
Excessive speed endangers yourself and other forest users.

Avoid Wheel Lock-up and Spin-out
Steep terrain is especially vulnerable to trail wear. Locking brakes on steep descents, or when stopping needlessly, damages trails. If a slope is steep enough to require locking wheels and skidding, dismount and walk your bicycle. Likewise, if an ascent is so steep your rear wheel slips and spins, dismount and walk your bicycle.

Protect Waterbars and Switchbacks
Waterbars, the rock and log drains built to direct water off trails, protect trails from erosion. When you encounter a waterbar, ride directly over the top or dismount and walk your bicycle. Riding around the ends of water-bars destroys them and speeds erosion. Skidding around switchback corners shortens trail life. Slow down for switchback corners and keep your wheels rolling.

If You Abuse It, You Lose It
Mountain bikers are relative newcomers to the forest and must prove them-selves responsible trail users. By following the guidelines above, and by participating in trail maintenance service projects, bicyclists can help avoid closures which would prevent them from using trails.

I've never seen a better trail-etiquette list for mountain bikers. So have fun. Be careful. And don't screw up things for the next guy.

HITTING THE TRAIL

Once again, because this is a "where-to," not a "how-to" guide, the following will be brief. If you're a veteran trail rider these suggestions might serve to re-mind you of something you've forgotten to pack. If you're a newcomer, they might convince you to think twice before hitting the backcountry unprepared.

Water: I've heard the questions dozens of times. "How much is enough? One bottle? Two? Three?! But think of all that extra weight!" Well, one simple physio-logical fact should convince you to err on the side of excess when it comes to determining how much water to pack: a human working hard in ninety-degree temperature needs approximately ten quarts of fluids every day. Ten quarts. That's two and a half gallons—*twelve* large water bottles, or *sixteen* small ones. And with water weighing in at approximately eight pounds per gallon, a one-day supply comes to a whopping twenty pounds.

In other words, pack along two or three bottles even for short rides. And make sure you can purify the water found along the trail on longer routes. When writing of those routes where this could be of critical importance, each author has provided information on where water can be found near the trail—if it can be found at all. But drink it untreated and you run the risk of disease. [See *Giardia* in the Glossary.]

One sure way to kill both the bacteria and viruses in water is to boil it for ten minutes, plus one minute more for each one thousand feet of elevation above sea level. Right. That's just how you want to spend your time on a bike ride. Besides, who wants to carry a stove or denude the countryside stoking bonfires to boil water?

Luckily, there is a better way. Many riders pack along the effective, inexpensive, and only slightly distasteful tetraglycine hydroperiodide tablets (sold under the names of Potable Aqua, Globaline, Coughlan's, and others). Some invest in portable, lightweight purifiers that filter out the crud. Yes, purifying water with tablets or filters is a bother. But catch a case of Giardia sometime and you'll understand why it's worth the trouble.

Tools: Ever since my first cross-country tour in 1965, I've been kidded about the number of tools I pack on the trail. And so I will exit entirely from this discussion by providing a list compiled by two mechanic (and mountain biker) friends of mine. After all, since they make their living fixing bikes and get their kicks by riding them, who could be a better source?

The following is suggested as an absolute minimum:

> tire levers
> spare tube and patch kit
> air pump
> allen wrenches (3, 4, 5, and 6 mm)
> six-inch crescent (adjustable-end) wrench
> small flat-blade screwdriver
> chain rivet tool
> spoke wrench

In addition to the above, their personal tool pouches carried on the trail contain:

> channel locks (small)
> air gauge
> tire valve cap (the metal kind with a valve-stem remover)
> baling wire (approximately ten inches for temporary repairs)
> duct tape (small roll for temporary repairs or tire boot)
> boot material (small piece of old tire or a large tube patch)
> spare chain link
> rear derailleur pulley
> spare nuts and bolts
> paper towel and tube of waterless hand cleaner

First-aid kit: My personal kit contains the following, sealed inside double zip-lock bags:

sunshade
aspirin
butterfly-closure bandages
band-aids
gauze compress pads (a half-dozen 4″ × 4″)
gauze (1 roll)
ace bandages or Spenco joint wraps
Benadryl (an antihistamine to guard against possible allergic reactions)
water purification tablets
moleskin/Spenco "Second Skin"
hydrogen peroxide/iodine/Mercurochrome (some kind of antiseptic)
snakebite kit

Final considerations: The authors of this series have done a good job in suggesting that specific items be packed for certain trails—like raingear in particular seasons, a hat and gloves for mountain passes, or shades for desert jaunts. Heed their warnings, and think ahead. Good luck.

Dennis Coello
Salt Lake City

VERMONT

RIDE 1   *MOUNT SNOW*

Mount Snow is called "New England's Mountain Bike Capital"—and it is probably true. (Craftsbury Center in Craftsbury, Vermont, and the Greasey Wheel bike shop in Plymouth, New Hampshire, might wish to debate the point.) Mount Snow was the first large ski area in the region to promote mountain biking. Today, its Mountain Bike Center offers, for a modest fee, access to miles of ski trails, as well as information about self-guided rides on 140 miles of trails and dirt roads in the surrounding countryside. (One loop, the Johnson Hill/ Hathaway Trail, is described in this book.)

From Mount Snow you can do easy out-and-back rides on dirt roads, moderate loops on ski trails and dirt roads, or more difficult rides on secluded trails and roads that climb and descend for a mile or two. Mount Snow also offers a ski lift, guided tours, instruction, rentals, races, Saturday night parties, and lodging. Tours, instruction, rentals, the ski lift, and other packages are variously and reasonably priced.

General location: Just off VT 100 in West Dover.
Elevation change: Most rides include some climbing on trails or dirt roads, although the amount of climbing varies greatly.
Season: Riding is best from mid-June through the fall. Mud can dominate in spring.
Services: All the services listed above are available at the Mountain Bike Center, Mount Snow, on VT 100, 8 miles north of Wilmington. Call ahead for prices: (800) 245-7669. All other services are available along VT 100 just south of Mount Snow. Because this is ski resort country, there are plenty of overnight accommodations.
Hazards: Watch for typical obstructions along the trails: logs, loose rocks, and ruts. On the roads, watch for occasional vehicles.
Rescue index: You are never more than 2 miles from assistance.
Land status: Town roads and private ski trails.
Maps: Maps and ride sheets of many miles of trails and roads are available from the Mountain Bike Center at Mount Snow.
Finding the trail: Mount Snow ski resort allows mountain bikers to use its parking lot. Take VT 100 to the entrance for Mount Snow, 8 miles north of Wilmington. Turn left to Mount Snow; you'll soon reach a "T" junction with a sign "Handle Road" and arrows indicating various resort destinations. Follow signs for the mountain bike school. The mountain bike school, at present, is in the Main Base Lodge—a right and then a left turn. Upon arrival at the lodge, ask where you should park. If no one is there, park off of Handle Road.

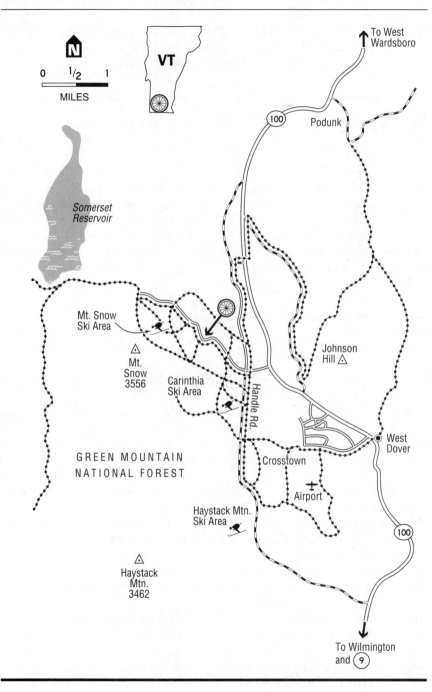

Sources of additional information: The Mountain Bike Center at Mount Snow, Vermont, (800) 245-7669.

Notes on the trail: The Mount Snow Mountain Bike Center has a "Trail Guide" and individual sheets describing particular rides. Many of these rides begin by going south on the paved Handle Road into the Crosstown Road area.

RIDE 2 *JOHNSON HILL / HATHAWAY TRAIL*

This challenging 12-mile loop alternates between secluded single- and double-track trails through the woods, and two-wheel-drive dirt and gravel roads through beautiful Vermont countryside. You head out from scenic Mount Snow, cruise along dirt roads, climb for a while, then enter woods, descend on a technical trail, and finish up in countryside with good views of nearby mountains. This ride links up with approximately 140 miles of trails and roads developed and maintained by the Mountain Bike Center at Mount Snow (see Sources of additional information).

General location: Just off VT 100 in West Dover.

Elevation change: You begin at about 1,900', climb to 2,200', and descend back to the beginning. There is some steep climbing on dirt roads, more gradual climbing on trails, and a screaming descent on a paved rural road.

Season: Riding is best from mid-June through the fall. Mud can dominate in spring.

Services: Water is available at a spigot outside the clubhouse at the Mount Snow golf course and also at a cabin in the woods (see the ride description suggested in "Notes on the trail"). All other services are available along VT 100 just south of Mount Snow. Because this is ski resort country, there are plenty of overnight accommodations. Guided tours, instruction, rentals, and maps of roads and trails are available from the Mountain Bike Center, Mount Snow, on VT 100, 8 miles north of Wilmington. (800) 245-7669.

Hazards: Watch for typical obstructions along the trails: logs, loose rocks, and ruts. On the roads, be aware of occasional vehicles and golfers.

Rescue index: You are never more than 2 miles from assistance.

Land status: Town roads and private ski trails.

Maps: Maps and ride sheets of many miles of trails and roads are available from the Mountain Bike Center at Mount Snow.

Finding the trail: Mount Snow ski resort allows mountain bikers to use its parking lot. Take VT 100 to the entrance for Mount Snow, 8 miles north of Wilmington. Turn left to Mount Snow; you'll soon reach a "T" junction with a sign "Handle Road" and arrows indicating various resort destinations. Follow the signs for the mountain bike school. The mountain bike school at present is in the

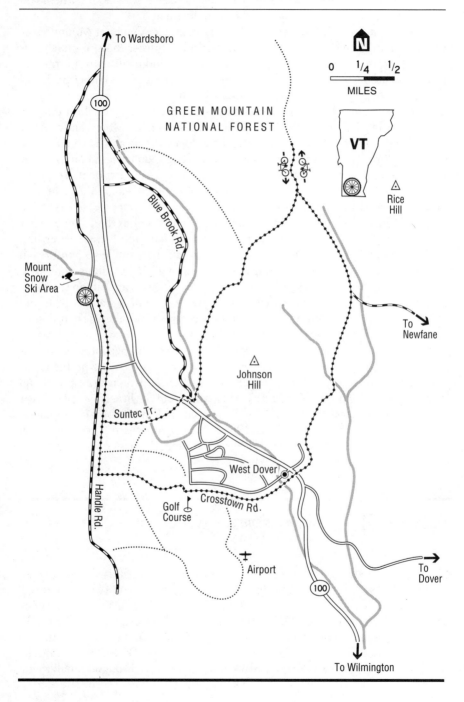

To Wardsboro

100

GREEN MOUNTAIN
NATIONAL FOREST

N

0   1/4   1/2
MILES

VT

Rice
Hill

Blue Brook Rd.

Mount
Snow
Ski Area

To
Newfane

Johnson
Hill

Suntec Tr.

West Dover

Golf
Course

Crosstown Rd.

Handle Rd.

Airport

To
Dover

100

To Wilmington

Main Base Lodge; make a right and then a left turn. Ask at the lodge where you should park. If no one is there park off of Handle Road.

Sources of additional information: The Mountain Bike Center at Mount Snow is a mountain biking mecca, offering guided tours, instruction, rentals, self-guided tours, races, and a map of trails and roads, including its own ski trails. A $5 fee buys access to the ski trails and Center. Tours, rentals, and other packages are also reasonably priced. Phone: (800) 245-7669.

Notes on the trail: Mount Snow Mountain Bike Center has a ride sheet that describes this ride in detail. Head south on Handle Road from Mount Snow. After about a mile, look for a sign on the left, "Over Some Rivers and Through Some Woods." Turn left, pass through a 4-way intersection, and after about another mile you will intersect Crosstown Road (another trail). Turn left on it. You soon reach a paved road. Veer right on the road, pass a golf course on the right, and continue down a steep hill.

Cross VT 100 at the bottom, climb, and fork right after less than a mile. After another mile, as the road veers sharply right, fork left onto a trail. After half a mile, at a small clearing, continue straight. In less than a mile you will reach another clearing with a sharp left turn. (Before turning left you might want to go straight for another mile or so until you reach a barrier with a cabin on the right. The barrier is for motorized vehicles; the owner is friendly toward cyclists and lets them use a water pump from a well between his two cabins. Then double back and turn right at the grassy junction.)

At a "T" junction, turn left then go straight at a fork. This becomes a challenging downhill that comes out of the woods at a private golf course on the right, veers left on Blue Brook Road, and meets VT 100. Turn right on VT 100 and immediately left onto gravel Stugger Road across from the fire department. Veer left, pass an electrical transformer, and come out at Kingswood Development. Bear right to reach the paved Handle Road. Turn right toward Mount Snow on Handle Road or veer onto ski trails on the left along the base of Mount Snow. (To use these trails you must first pay a $5 fee.)

RIDE 3   *WARDSBORO / NEWFANE*

This is a challenging 20-mile tour through woods, open countryside, and small towns. It has several miles of fairly steep climbing, mainly on two-wheel-drive roads, and some tough maneuvering on rugged and rocky trails. The ride can be connected with the Johnson Hill/Hathaway Trail ride by using other dirt roads, or shortened by skipping a self-contained five-mile loop in the middle of it.

About half of the ride is on maintained dirt roads, the other half on double-track trails. Along the way you see panoramic views, pass through a small town,

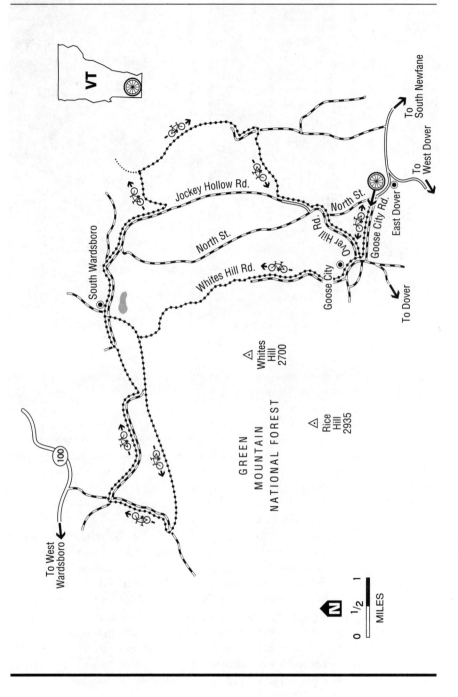

A stretch of technical climbing. Wardsboro, Vermont.

and ride by wildflowers, stone walls, and wild blackberry and raspberry bushes whose berries ripen in late summer.

General location: Five miles east of VT 100, beginning outside East Dover.
Elevation change: This ride has plenty of climbing, mainly on two-wheel-drive dirt roads, and a lot of descending, mainly on trails. It begins at 1,300′, climbs to 2,100′, descends to 1,500′, climbs again to 1,900′, and descends to 1,300′. After an initial climb of about 2 miles, no climb is longer than a mile.
Season: Mid-June through fall is best for riding. As usual, unpaved roads and trails in New England can be muddy in the spring.
Services: All services are available along VT 100 and in Wilmington. Because this is ski resort country, there are plenty of overnight accommodations with more reasonable rates during the off-season. Guided tours, instruction, rentals, and maps of roads and trails are available from the Mountain Bike Center, Mount Snow, on VT 100, 8 miles north of Wilmington. (800) 245-7669.
Hazards: Some trails can be "greasy" during wet weather, requiring more riding concentration. Also, some trails contain the usual minor obstructions: loose rocks, ruts, and some mud. Finally, watch out for occasional traffic on the two-wheel-drive roads, especially when descending.
Rescue index: You are never more than 2 miles from assistance.

Land status: Town roads, old town roads, and public trails.

Maps: Maps and ride sheets of about 140 miles of interconnecting trails and dirt roads are available from the Mountain Bike Center at Mount Snow. Most of this route also appears in *The Vermont Atlas and Gazetteer* (DeLorme Mapping Co., Freeport, Maine), which is available at many stores.

Finding the trail: On VT 100, 3.8 miles north of the junction of VT 100 and VT 9 in Wilmington, turn at a sign for "Dover/East Dover/Newfane" (from the south it's a right turn). After several miles you go through East Dover, fork left uphill, and then left downhill after one-third of a mile. Park anywhere on the left side of the road—and lock up.

Sources of additional information: The Mountain Bike Center in Mount Snow on VT 100, 8 miles north of Wilmington, is a mountain biking mecca offering guided tours, instruction, rentals, self-guided tours, races, and a map of trails and roads, including its own ski trails. A $5 fee buys access to the ski trails and center. Tours, rentals, and other packages are also reasonably priced. Phone: (800) 245-7669.

Notes on the trail: This long ride has many turns, especially in the second half, so be alert and consult a good map. Begin by riding up the road, which climbs steadily and becomes steeper. Bear left at a fork after a half-mile, go downhill on Rock River Road, and turn right after some three-quarters of a mile, then immediately left onto Whites Hill Road. After another couple of miles fork left onto a jeep trail, which soon veers sharply to the left, and then right. (If a small bridge over the brook has collapsed, take a short detour around it on the right.)

You will come to an intersection. Turn left; you'll pass a small clearing on the left and a narrower trail going uphill on the right. To do a shorter 15-mile ride, turn right up the trail. Otherwise, turn left through the clearing and pick up a trail into the woods. There is a severely eroded downhill section on this trail, with a detour path paralleling it on the right side. After a stream crossing, turn right at a fork with three red dots on a tree. You will come out on a two-wheel-drive road with a cabin on the left. Turn right, and at the next intersection take a hard right, crossing a bridge. Keep to the right and go steadily uphill. You will reach the clearing again where you had the option of turning up the jeep trail. This time turn up the trail (now on the left), and after a short distance, you'll see a field on the right with a scenic view. It's a good place to take a break.

Stay to the right and enter South Wardsboro. Veer to the right through town, fork right at a grassy island, then left onto a dirt road and right onto a narrower road. On a downhill turn onto a jeep trail on the left, then right onto another trail. You come out on a road. Just before the road bends to the right, turn right sharply up a trail. You will come out on another two-wheel-drive road. Turn left on it, climb to a panoramic view on the left, and veer left on pavement, then right. Take a right fork and, after a long steep hill, you will reach a "T" junction. Turn left, then stay to the left, and you will be back on the dirt road you pedaled up.

RIDE 4 *PUTNEY MOUNTAIN*

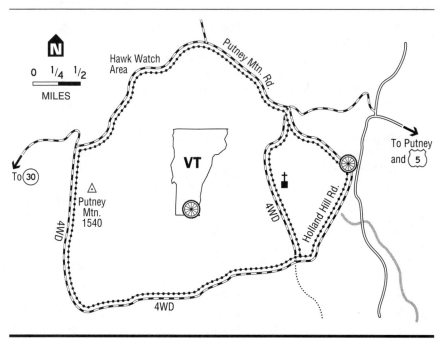

RIDE 4 *PUTNEY MOUNTAIN*

This seven-mile loop begins on a two-wheel-drive dirt road that passes homes in small clearings, long stone walls, and quiet ponds to complete the classic New England setting. Soon, though, you enter a more secluded landscape of birch-filled woods and old orchards. The ride alternates between these two habitats.

About two-thirds of the ride is on two-wheel-drive dirt roads, while the other third is on four-wheel-drive roads. There's a fair amount of climbing, alternating with flat and downhill stretches. Spreading out to the north and west of this ride are many more miles of dirt roads.

General location: Just outside Putney.
Elevation change: A steady, moderately steep climb of about 1 mile is followed by a flat and downhill section for another mile or two, a half mile of climbing, and about 3 miles on flat and downhill terrain.
Season: The best riding is from about June to October.

Services: Putney is a recreational and cultural center in southern Vermont, with country stores and down-home eateries. The West Hill Bike Shop on Depot Road, (802) 387-5718, specializes in mountain biking.

Hazards: Watch for occasional traffic on the two-wheel-drive dirt roads, especially when you are descending.

Rescue index: You will be no more than a mile from a traveled road or home.

Land status: Town roads and old town roads.

Maps: *The Vermont Atlas and Gazetteer* (DeLorme Mapping Co., Freeport, Maine), a collection of maps showing all byways in the state, is available in many stores.

Finding the trail: Take Exit 4 on Interstate 91, and head toward Putney on US 5. In the middle of Putney, fork left off US 5, toward Westhill. After 1 mile turn left uphill toward Putney School. Take the right fork at 1.3 miles, veer left at 2 miles, and turn right onto Putney Mountain Road at 2.3 miles, parking on wide turnoffs on either side of the road.

Sources of additional information: The West Hill Shop on Depot Road in Putney (RR2, Box 35, Putney, Vermont, 05346) has a lot of information about this and other rides in the area. Phone: (802) 387-5718.

Notes on the trail: Turn left immediately at the bottom of Putney Mountain Road, onto Holland Hill Road. Climb for about a mile, reaching a "T" junction before a stone wall and a large house. Turn right, and after a couple of hundred feet, turn right again onto a narrower dirt road. After six-tenths of a mile, the road becomes four-wheel-drive. Veer right at an upcoming junction and come out on Putney Mountain Road.

Turn left, pass a sign for Banning Road on the right, and after 2.3 miles, while going downhill and just before a sharp right turn, take a sharp, steep left turn up a narrow road. Continue on this road until it reaches a left turn on another two-wheel-drive road. After 1.7 miles on this road, you will come back to the "T" junction at the stone wall and large house. Ride back down Holland Hill Road or turn left and reach Putney Mountain Road, turning right to descend.

RIDE 5 *LANDGROVE*

This 11.5-mile loop through scenic countryside could be a ride conducted by one of the several bike touring organizations in Vermont. Rolling along these two-wheel-drive dirt roads you will experience a classic New England landscape: rolling fields bordered by stone walls, small bridges across streams, clusters of well-maintained homes, a swimming hole or two, and woods of oak, maple, and aspen.

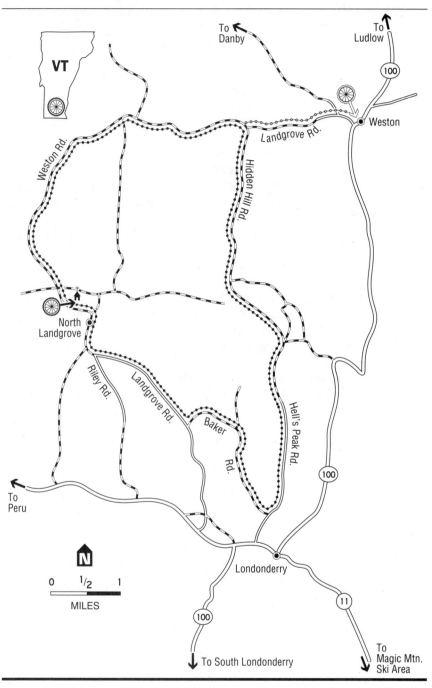

General location: The ride passes through Landgrove, Londonderry, and Weston.

Elevation change: The terrain along this ride is rolling, with occasional not-too-steep climbing and descending on dirt roads.

Season: You can do this ride in any season.

Services: All services are available in Weston and Londonderry. Accommodations in a clapboard farmhouse in Londonderry: (802) 824-3933. A bike shop: Barney's on VT103 in Chester: (802) 875-3517.

Hazards: None except for occasional traffic.

Rescue index: This ride regularly passes by houses.

Land status: Town roads.

Maps: A state road map will do, or pick up *The Vermont Atlas and Gazetteer* (DeLorme Mapping Co., Freeport, Maine), available in many stores.

Finding the trail: Depending on how far you want to ride, you can begin this tour with an out-and-back stretch from either Weston or Peru. Or begin on the loop. From VT 100 in Weston, turn left just before the green, pass a school on the left, cross a bridge, and turn left again. You will climb steeply before the road becomes dirt. Follow Weston Road for about 5 miles until you reach a handsome white municipal building on the left, just before an intersection, with a sign on it: "Town of Landgrove, Chartered 1780." Park in front of this historic building. You can also reach this site from VT 11 in Peru.

Sources of additional information: Chamber of Commerce, Londonderry, (802) 824-8178, has general information on the entire area and stocks a 24-hour information booth at the junction of VT100 and VT11.

Notes on the trail: Head south through an intersection, and turn right at a "T" junction, cross a concrete bridge, and ride past several homes. Turn left at an intersection onto pavement. After about a mile, watch for a left turn just past a field and before a small pond on the left. Turn left there and head downhill, crossing a bridge and stream with a swimming hole. Be sure to check out the view of a mountain ahead. Then turn right at an intersection, and reach a paved road after 1 mile. Turn left on the pavement, which becomes dirt after 1 mile. At the next intersection turn left uphill, then take a right fork after a half mile. After about 2 miles you reach a "T" junction. Turn left and follow Weston Road for about 4 miles, staying to the right.

RIDE 6   *WESTON*

This 14-mile loop rolls over two-wheel-drive unpaved roads through classic Vermont countryside. There is some short climbing, one steep descent, and a mile-long section on a jeep road. Along the way you pass handsome homes (including

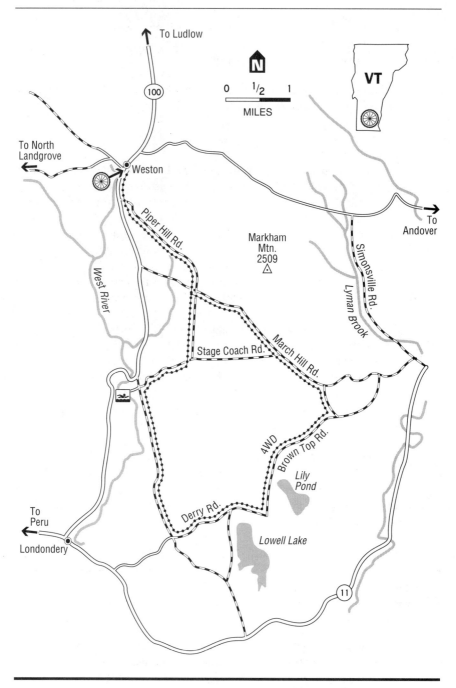

To Ludlow

N

0   1/2   1

MILES

VT

To North
Landgrove

Weston

100

Piper Hill Rd.

West River

Markham
Mtn.
2509

Simonsville Rd.

Lyman Brook

To
Andover

Stage Coach Rd.

March Hill Rd.

4WD

Brown Top Rd.

Lily
Pond

Lowell Lake

To
Peru

Londondery

Derry Rd.

11

Classic Vermont architecture. Weston, Vermont.

one brightly colored home that's a remodeled schoolhouse), farms with animals grazing in fields, stone walls, several streams, pine woods, and mountains on the horizon. This route can be connected with the Landgrove ride.

The ride begins and ends in a lively small town. You might want to spend some time sightseeing there. Weston has several country stores, a museum of "Vermontiana," a bowl-making mill, and stores offering homemade ice cream. After riding and sight-seeing, relax and eat and drink at the gazebo on the village green.

General location: The ride passes through the towns of Weston and Londonderry.
Elevation change: This is rolling terrain, with a couple of short, moderately steep climbs.
Season: This can be a 4-season ride. There is some mud in the spring.
Services: All services are available in Weston and Londonderry. Bike Shop:

Barney's on VT103 in Chester: (802) 875-3517.

Hazards: Near the beginning of the ride, on Stage Coach Road, there is a short, steep, winding downhill, which requires braking skill. And always watch out for oncoming vehicles.

Rescue index: You are always near homes on this ride.

Land status: Active town roads.

Maps: A detailed state road map will do, or pick up The Vermont Atlas and *Gazetter* (DeLorme Mapping Co., Freeport, Maine), available in many stores.

Finding the trail: The ride begins in the town of Weston on VT 100.

Sources of additional information: Chamber of Commerce, Londonderry, (802) 824-8178, has general information on the entire area and stocks a 24-hour information booth at the junction of VT 100 and VT 11.

Notes on the trail: Head out of Weston southward on VT 100, and after four-tenths of a mile turn left up a paved road, then bear right and left. After about another mile go straight at an intersection with a stop sign at it. At the next intersection, turn right onto Stage Coach Road and descend. At the bottom turn left on a dirt road. Or you might want to take a short side trip: head straight on the pavement and onto a playing field (soccer and polo). On the right side of the field you'll reach a swimming hole along the river.

After a couple of miles going south, turn left on Derry Road. The road begins to climb, becomes four-wheel-drive, and passes an abandoned camp—Camp Derry. Fork to the left, and after eight-tenths of a mile turn left. Take another left fork after another four-tenths of a mile, and immediately another left. After another half mile, bear right, and turn right at the stop sign. You are heading back toward Weston. When you reach pavement stay to the right, intersecting VT 100. Turn right to reach Weston.

RIDE 7 *MOUNT TABOR / DANBY ROAD*

You can ride out and back for 20 miles (round-trip) on this secluded gravel road, located entirely in the Green Mountain National Forest. Although it is well maintained, along its borders you will pass only light woods, clearings of new growth, wildlife, a stream paralleling the road for five miles, and an occasional vehicle.

Get a workout, practice your cadence, or enjoy the scenery along this route, which crosses several popular trails, including one that heads north to Little Rock Pond, a popular swimming spot. There's also a picnic area at the road's western end.

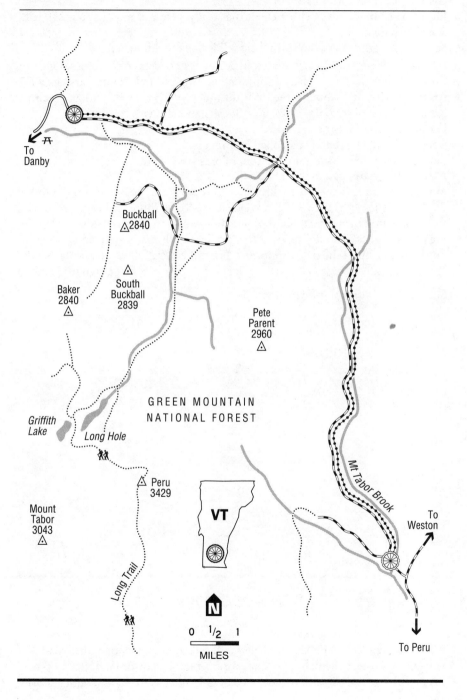

To Danby

Buckball
△2840

Baker
2840
△

South
Buckball
2839
△

Pete
Parent
2960
△

GREEN MOUNTAIN
NATIONAL FOREST

*Griffith
Lake*

Long Hole

△ Peru
3429

Mount
Tabor
3043
△

Mt Tabor Brook

To
Weston

VT

Long Trail

To Peru

0   1/2   1

N

MILES

General location: Mount Tabor.

Elevation change: From either end it is a steady, gentle climb of about 250 feet, and then a descent.

Season: Any time between spring and fall is fine for riding here.

Services: All services are available in Manchester Center, 20 miles south of Mount Tabor on VT 7. There is camping at Emerald Lake State Park on VT 7 south of Mount Tabor. Green Mountain Cyclery (133 Strongs Avenue, Rutland, Vermont 05701, (802) 775-0869) can help with repairs.

Hazards: None except for an occasional vehicle.

Rescue index: The road is patrolled by rangers.

Land status: Green Mountain National Forest road.

Maps: Any state road map will do.

Finding the trail: The ride is a bit easier to reach from the western end. On VT 7 ("Ethan Allen Highway") look for signs for Mount Tabor and Danby. Coming from the south, turn right toward Mount Tabor just after several industrial buildings, at a sign for Mount Tabor. After 3 miles you'll reach a paved parking lot on the right, inside the national forest. (From the east, follow directions for the Landgrove ride, except that you turn right off Weston Road at a sign for Danby.)

Sources of additional information:

Manchester Ranger District
Green Mountain National Forest
Routes 11 and 30, Box 1940
Manchester Center, VT 05255
(802) 362-2307

RIDE 8   *SOUTH WOODSTOCK*

This is a technically challenging seven-mile ride that climbs on a dirt road to a rugged trail—and then climbs some more. At the height-of-land, the loop connects with many more miles of secluded double-track trails to the south and west

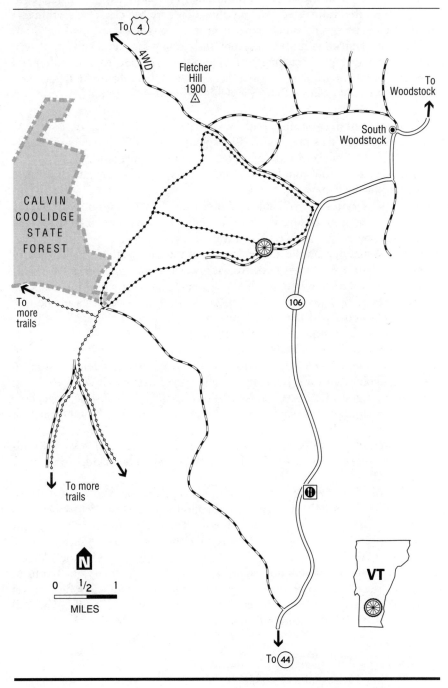

To ④

4WD

Fletcher
Hill
1900

To
Woodstock

South
Woodstock

CALVIN
COOLIDGE
STATE
FOREST

To
more
trails

106

To more
trails

N

0   1/2   1

MILES

VT

To ㊹

of it. Carry a map and compass if you decide to do more exploring. The two-mile climb on the trail is steep and gnarly—don't try to "clean" everything. It also crosses water several times; expect wetness in any season.

While you're tackling the ascent, enjoy the rushing stream next to it, as well as the lush foliage. After reaching the height-of-land the ride becomes softer and less rocky, before descending steeply on a two-wheel-drive dirt road. If you want to sightsee, visit Woodstock, which is full of stores and restaurants.

General location: Just outside South Woodstock.

Elevation change: This ride gains 800′, beginning at 1,100′, and climbs steadily to 1,900′ on the trail; it then descends on a maintained dirt road.

Season: Riding is good from June through fall. Expect a fair amount of wetness during the spring.

Services: All services are available in Woodstock. To the south on VT 106, the Hammondsville Store & Snack Bar in Reading has provisions. Bike shop: The Cyclery Plus on Route 4 in West Woodstock.

Hazards: Depending on the amount of recent rainfall, you may have to carry your bike across a small stream or two or a washed-out area—or at least slow down to plan your line of attack. On the descent, watch for oncoming traffic.

Rescue index: You will be no more than 2 miles from traveled roads and homes.

Land status: Active and abandoned town roads.

Maps: USGS, Woodstock, South, VT (1966).

Finding the trail: From Woodstock take VT 106 South, passing through South Woodstock after 4.7 miles. Turn left sharply onto VT 106 and continue for 1.6 miles, until you reach a dirt road on the right with signs: "Noah Wood Rd." and "Legal Load Limit 14,000 lbs." This is the trailhead. Park on a wide gravel area next to the road. From the south, the road is about 6 miles north of the junction of VT 106 and VT 44.

Sources of additional information: The Cyclery Plus on Route 4 in West Woodstock, Vermont, services mountain bikes, and can suggest other rides in the area. Phone: (802) 457-3377.

Notes on the trail: Fork left after four-tenths of a mile on Noah Wood Road. (You might try the inviting trail on the right another time. The left fork becomes a trail too.) After passing several more houses, you're on a rocky trail for about 2 miles. You will reach a junction on the right, opposite a tree with several snowmobile signs on it: "So. Woodstock," "Hartland," and "W. Windsor." Watch carefully for this turnoff and turn right, cross a stream, and turn right at a fork. Continue veering right on rolling, grassy terrain until you come out on a gravel road after about a mile. Turn right and head downhill for over 2 miles. You will come out on VT 106 one-third mile north of Noah Wood Road.

RIDE 9   *TURNPIKE ROAD*

This 15-mile loop is at the center of many miles of unpaved roads fanning north of Norwich, between the Connecticut and White Rivers. It begins on pavement in Norwich for two and a half miles, then heads steadily and gently uphill on a hard-packed dirt road, which becomes narrower and more rugged, finally turning into a double-track trail. The return trip alternates between two-wheel-drive country roads and a jeep trail.

This ride can't decide whether it should be a leisurely tour through well-appointed countryside—handsome homes and farms, fields, orchards, and streams—or a technical trek on secluded trails. It's a hybrid ride.

General location: Norwich, with short stretches in the adjoining towns of Sharon, Strafford, and Thetford.

Elevation change: The ride begins at 800' and climbs steadily and gently to 1,600' before descending.

Season: Summer and fall are best for riding, but the fairly well-drained terrain makes this a good spring ride, too.

Services: All services are available in Norwich, including food and drink at Dan and Whit's grocery store on Main Street.

Hazards: Watch out for light traffic on the two-wheel-drive roads and the usual minor obstructions on jeep trails.

Rescue index: You are never more than 1.5 miles from traveled roads.

Land status: Town roads and abandoned town roads.

Maps: A detailed state map will do, or pick up *The Vermont Atlas and Gazetteer* (DeLorme Mapping Co., Freeport, Maine), which shows all roads in the state.

Finding the trail: Norwich is off Interstate 91, 6 miles north of its junction with Interstate 89, and 3 miles north of White River Junction. This attractive community is just across the Connecticut River from Hanover, New Hampshire, the home of Dartmouth College. Park in town.

Sources of additional information:

> Omer & Bob's Sportshop
> 7 Allen Street
> Hanover, New Hampshire 03755
> (603) 643-3525

> Tom Mowatt Cycles
> Olde Nugget Alley
> Hanover, New Hampshire 03755
> (603) 643-5522

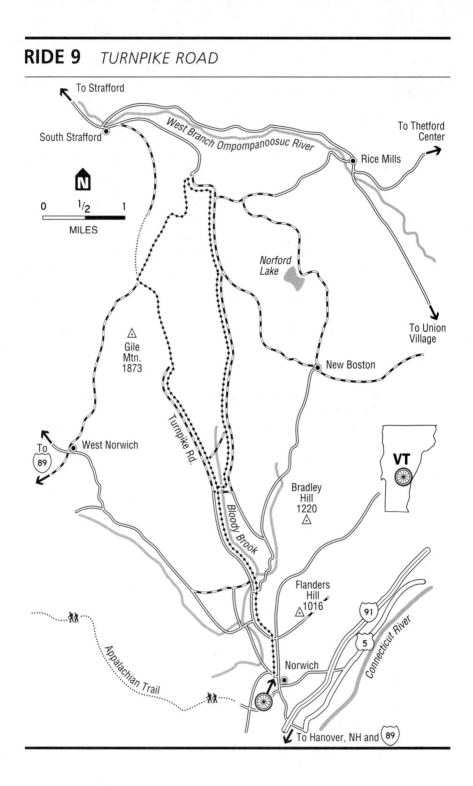

Notes on the trail: Take Main Street north out of Norwich for a half mile and turn left on Turnpike Road. Fork left after another mile. Pavement turns to dirt, and after climbing gently for about 3 miles, the road heads straight into the woods on a trail. After three-quarters of a mile take a right fork in the woods; after another 2 miles the trail comes out on a two-wheel-drive dirt road. Turn right, and stay to the right at a fork after about a half mile. Here comes the tricky turn. A mile past the last fork, turn up a dirt road (with two mailboxes) that looks like a driveway. After several hundred yards, the road seems to go straight into the front yard of a modest house. You can ride through the yard to pick up an abandoned road just beyond. This trail comes out on another two-wheel-drive dirt road at a farm. After 1.5 miles take a right fork, then veer sharply right downhill at a scenic view and farmhouse. You reach a "T" junction at Turnpike Road. Turn left toward Norwich.

RIDE 10   *UNION VILLAGE DAM RECREATION AREA*

This attractive linear park has a two-and-a-half-mile path running through it, which makes a pleasant, leisurely 5-mile out-and-back ride. It's especially good for casual riders, youths, and families. Along one side of the park is a gorge with a river in it, clearings with picnic tables, a wooden bridge, and scenic views across the gorge.

At the southern end of the ride stands impressive Union Village Dam, which you can ride across for a panoramic view of the countryside. The 170-foot-high, 1,100-foot-long dam was built in 1950 for a mere four million dollars.

General location: Between the towns of Thetford Center and Union Village.
Elevation change: The route is flat with occasional short hills and an optional short, steep climb to reach the dam.
Season: High, well-drained terrain makes this a good ride for spring, while the surrounding woods make it pleasantly shady in summer and colorful in fall.
Services: All services are available in Thetford Center to the north and Norwich to the south. There is camping in Thetford State Park, just to the east.
Hazards: Watch out for other park users.
Rescue index: The park is patrolled.
Land status: Public park road.
Maps: A detailed state road map will show the area.
Finding the trail: From Interstate 91, take VT 113 west for 1.8 miles. Coming into Thetford Center on a steep downhill, just before a sign on the left ("Thetford Center"), you'll see a small white sign (also on the left) that reads "Recreation Center." Turn left into the park; there's a parking lot a few hundred feet on the left.

RIDE 10 *UNION VILLAGE DAM RECREATION AREA*

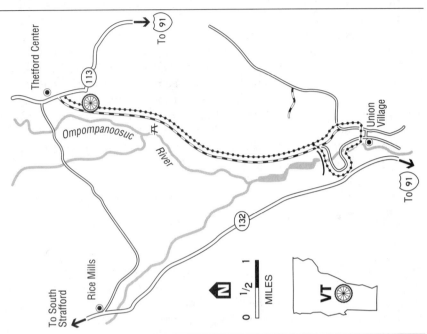

Sources of additional information: If you have any trouble finding the park, ask anyone in the towns of Union Village or Thetford.

Notes on the trail: To extend this ride for a mile or so (by climbing a hill or two), head up the steep, paved stretch of road at the dam. Then, instead of turning right across the dam itself, fork left past a brick building. After another three-tenths of a mile you will come out on a paved road. Turn right, and head downhill steeply, bearing right across a covered bridge and turning right again. You will reenter the Union Village Dam area riding steeply uphill. When you reach the far side of the dam, turn right, cross the dam, then turn left to return to Thetford.

RIDE 11 *SABLE MOUNTAIN*

This fairly challenging eight-mile loop runs through both open countryside and deep woods. You're on a backcountry road for a mile, rolling past vistas, fields of wildflowers, an old cemetery, and if you're lucky, a grazing deer. Then it's time to leave behind even this secluded setting for a rugged trail and old roads through woods, accompanied by a roaring brook.

Old road in Union Village Dam Recreation Area (dam is on the right in background). Union Village, Vermont.

For most of the ride you're in the woods, away from all signs of civilization except a cabin or two. Be prepared to climb occasionally, mostly on graded dirt roads. And there's a fun and challenging descent for a mile on a rock-strewn double-track trail.

General location: Two miles south of Pittsfield on VT 100.
Elevation change: This ride begins at 1,900', climbs to 2,100', drops steeply to 1,100', and then climbs more gradually to 1,900'. The total elevation gain is 1,000'.
Season: You can do this ride anytime between mid-June and fall.
Services: All services are available in Pittsfield and along VT 100.
Hazards: Make sure your brakes (and you) are in good working order before making the 1-mile descent on the eroded, loose rock trail just after the initial climb.
Rescue index: You will be about 2 miles from inhabited houses.
Land status: Old town roads.
Maps: Green Mountain Bicycle Service in Rochester has a wall of topographic maps and some photocopies.

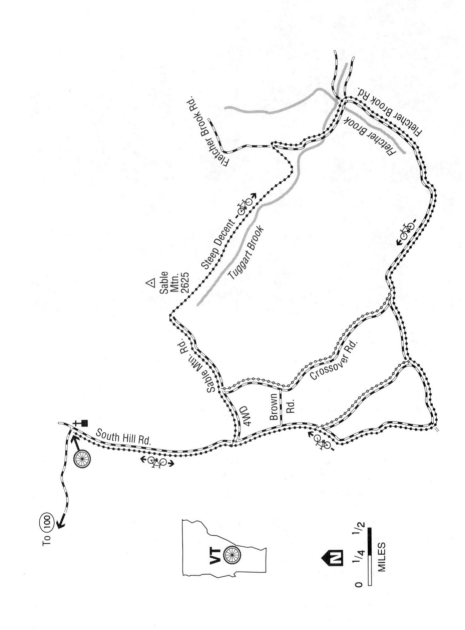

An inn that caters to mountain bicyclists. Pittsfield, Vermont.

Finding the trail: The ride begins on South Hill Road. From Pittsfield head south, then turn left off VT 100 after 2.4 miles. Climb, fork left, and park at a "T" junction just before South Hill Road, about 2 miles from VT 100.

Sources of additional information: Green Mountain Bicycle Service, Box 253, Rochester, VT 05767, (802) 767-4464. This is a full-service mountain bike outfit.

Notes on the trail: Begin by turning right at the "T" junction on South Hill Road. Ride past an old cemetery on the left, rolling along this rural road for 1.1 miles. Turn left up the four-wheel-drive Sable Mountain Road on the left (marked "ATV traveled road"). If you pass a road on the left marked "Brown Rd./ATV traveled road" just before a clearing, you've gone slightly too far on South Hill Road. Climb the first road, forking right on it, and then veer right. You will descend on a rocky trail for a mile and hear the rushing of Fletcher Brook. After riding uphill for a short distance you will reach a "T" junction at the two-wheel-drive Fletcher Brook Road. Turn right, and go downhill to a junction of 3 roads. Turn onto the far right road (marked "Lost Acre Road/ATV traveled"). Climb next to the brook for over a mile, until you pass the Lost Acre campsite on the right and reach a fork. Fork left on an overgrown road marked "Road Closed." After a while you will reach a newer campsite on the right. Fork left again, and then turn right uphill. (The last left fork is a new road, owned by International Paper, with a gate farther up the road.) The left-hand road becomes South Hill Road, heading north. (On the southeastern stretch of the ride you could take either of the two right forks, instead of the left ones. The first one becomes Brown Road, which joins South Hill Road just south of the first turnoff. The second old road is a shortcut to South Hill Road.)

RIDE 12 *MICHIGAN ROAD*

This six-mile loop is made up of two distinct halves: a gentle climb on a narrow two-wheel-drive road and a gradual descent on a more challenging woods trail. You can extend the ride by beginning in Pittsfield, which adds another four miles on secluded, two-wheel-drive dirt roads, the last two miles along a scenic river.

On the first half you gradually leave civilization behind, entering the Green Mountain National Forest on a secluded road lined with wildflowers, wild berry bushes, and light woods. On the trail you cross a brook and pass a secluded meadow or two. Afterward, relax in attractive Pittsfield.

General location: Just east of Pittsfield off VT 100.

Elevation change: This ride is a steady, gradual climb from 1,300' to 2,100' before descending.

Season: Mid-June through fall is the best riding time. Expect mud in spring.

Services: All services are available in Pittsfield.

Hazards: Be prepared for an abrupt change at the midpoint of this ride, switching from a smooth dirt road to a rugged trail with some obstructions: rocks, mud holes, logs, and water bars. Depending on weather conditions, there can also be mosquitoes in the woods.

Rescue index: You will never be more than about 3 miles from assistance.

Land status: An active town road, a Green Mountain National Forest road, and an abandoned town road.

Maps: Green Mountain Bicycle Service in Rochester has a wall of topographical maps and some photocopies.

Finding the trail: You can begin riding at the Pittsfield General Store in Pittsfield, on VT 100, or from a parking area up Upper Michigan Road. From the general store on VT 100 in Pittsfield turn on Upper Michigan Road; you will reach a parking area on the left after 2.3 miles.

Sources of additional information: Green Mountain Bicycle Service, Box 253, Rochester, VT 05767, (802) 767-4464. This is a full-service mountain bike outfit.

Notes on the trail: Upper Michigan Road is easy to follow. Just stay to the left,

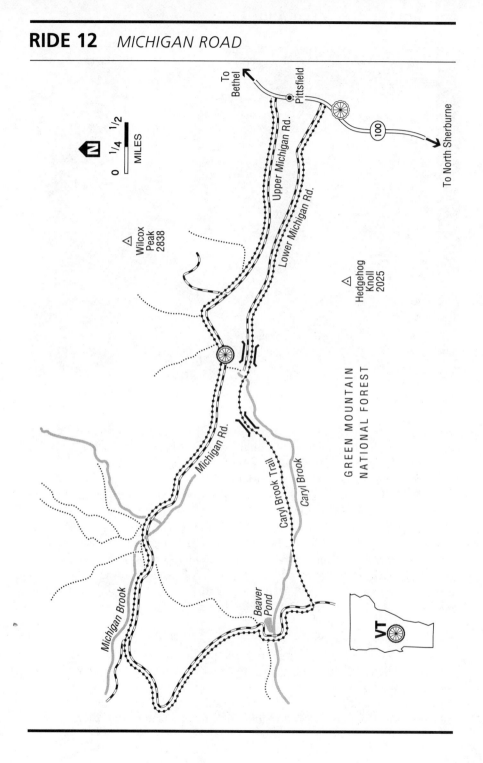

To Bethel

Pittsfield

To North Sherburne

100

Upper Michigan Rd.

Lower Michigan Rd.

Wilcox
Peak
2838

Hedgehog
Knoll
2025

N

0   ¼   ½

MILES

Michigan Rd.

Caryl Brook Trail

Caryl Brook

GREEN MOUNTAIN
NATIONAL FOREST

Michigan Brook

Beaver
Pond

VT

A pastoral road through the Green Mountain National Forest. Pittsfield, Vermont.

and avoid a couple of dead-end right turns, and it turns into a secluded grassy road, passing through a Green Mountain National Forest gate about 2.5 miles from the parking area. After another mile the road passes a beaver pond on the left, and after another half mile you reach an overgrown trail on the left—Caryl Brook Trail. If you miss it you'll soon reach the end of the road; turn back a few hundred yards to find the trail.

Follow the trail through the woods. If you're not returning to VT 100, the easiest way to find the cutoff trail that joins Upper Michigan Road is to reach a second large wooden bridge with an unpaved road beyond it. Turn back and find the cutoff (now on the right) a few hundred feet before the bridge. You might have to carry your bike for a short distance up this short, steep trail, which comes out on Upper Michigan Road, just above the parking area.

NOTE: *Green Mountain National Forest.* This 325,000-acre forest has over 500 miles of trails. The forest includes half the public land in Vermont, as well as land owned by utility and timber companies and individuals. At present off-road biking is not allowed on the popular Appalachian Trail and Long Trail. Bikes are permitted on logging roads and less-used trails. Because the Green Mountains are more rideable than the White Mountains in New Hampshire, Green Mountain forest officials are more sensitive to the overuse of trails. As usual, cyclists should slow down around any hikers and equestrians, and avoid delicate trails.

For information about the southern half of the forest, contact: Manchester Ranger District, Green Mountain National Forest, Routes 11 and 30, Box 1940, Manchester Center, Vermont, 05255, (802) 362-2307. The northern half is managed by the Middlebury Ranger District, GMNF, Route 7, Box 1260, Middlebury, Vermont, 05753, (802) 388-4362; and the Rochester Ranger District, GMNF, Route 100, Box 108, Rochester, Vermont, 05767, (802) 767-4777.

RIDE 13 *BINGO ROAD*

This easy out-and-back ride rolls for four and a half miles into the Green Mountain National Forest on a gravel and dirt road. To extend the ride, begin in quaint Rochester on a scenic paved road. Also, several narrower, more rugged trails fan off from Bingo Road.

This is a secluded, gently sloping dead-end road that parallels a babbling brook. Each season here has its attractions: spring wildflowers, early summer swimming holes, fall blackberries and raspberries, the brilliant reds and oranges of shedding deciduous trees, and winter evergreens and white stillness. Look for cellar holes and old apple trees in the woods, and enjoy the classic Vermont landscape in and out of Rochester.

General location: 4 miles west of Rochester on VT 73.
Elevation change: It's a steady, gentle climb gaining about 500'. Side trails climb another 300' or so.
Season: This is a 4-season ride.
Services: All services are located in attractive Rochester, including a bike shop, American Youth Hostel lodge (for all ages), a good bed-and-breakfast inn managed by mountain bikers, and inexpensive restaurants.
Hazards: None.
Rescue index: Bingo Road is a secluded but easily traversed road, not far from well traveled roads.
Land status: Bingo Road enters the Green Mountain National Forest. Cyclists are allowed on the fire roads in this vast forest, but not on some single-track trails, especially the popular Appalachian Trail and Long Trail.
Maps: USGS maps are stocked at the National Forest Service office in Rochester. *The Vermont Atlas and Gazetteer* (DeLorme Mapping Co.) is available in many bookstores and shops. The Green Mountain Bicycle Service in Rochester also has maps and can offer advice.
Finding the trail: You can park either in Rochester or along Bingo Road. From

RIDE 13 *BINGO ROAD*

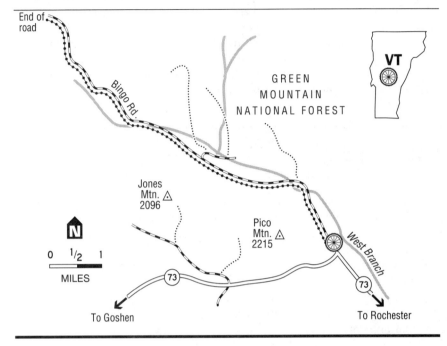

Rochester head south on VT 100, and take a right turn onto VT 73, traveling for about 3.5 miles. When VT 73, traveling veers sharply to the left, go straight on unpaved Bingo Road. Park off the road.

Sources of additional information:

> Green Mountain National Forest Office
> Rochester Ranger District
> VT 100, RD 1, Box 108
> Rochester, Vermont 05767
> (802) 767-4777

> Green Mountain Bicycle Service
> P.O. Box 253
> Rochester, Vermont 05767
> (802) 767-4464
> Located in the center of quaint Rochester on VT 100, this small business rents, repairs, and sells mountain bikes. It also specializes in guiding individuals and groups on leisurely, or more challenging, excursions. Drop in for a chat.

A mountain bike shop owner and tour guide. Rochester, Vermont.

The Huntington House Inn on the Green in Rochester, (802) 767-4868, is owned by a mountain biker.

Notes on the trail: Bingo Road goes into the Green Mountain National Forest for 4.5 miles, ending at a cul-de-sac. After riding for a couple of miles, you can explore one of several off-shooting short loops. Pine Brook Trail comes up on the right after about 2.5 miles. Approximately a mile long, it climbs on a gravel road and descends back to Bingo Road. Just before the third cement bridge on Bingo Road, a trail on the left heads off toward a waterfall and beaver pond. If you can reach the other side of the pond, the trail loops back to VT 73.

RIDE 14 *ROCHESTER / NORTH HOLLOW*

You can ride approximately 5 to 30 miles on back roads along this scenic ridge. After climbing from Rochester, head north for a longer ride or south for a shorter one. Return to Rochester by descending to scenic, paved VT 100, or by doubling back. Be ready to do some climbing on smooth dirt roads. Once you're on the ridge, you can crank along at a fast pace or take in the scenery: silver-sided barns and farms, fields with grazing animals, colorful foliage, and edible berries in the fall.

Along the way you might visit several sites. Two miles north of Rochester, turn west on Quarry Road to reach a working marble quarry. In Granville (ten miles north of Rochester) there's scenic Granville Reservation, which contains Moss Glen Falls. A three-mile side trip off VT 100, on VT 125 East, will bring you to Texas Falls. Or cool off at a swimming hole near the bridge just north of Rochester on VT 100.

General location: Rochester, north of the intersection of VT 100 and VT 73.
Elevation change: Rochester is located at 900'. The ride begins with a moderately steep climb of 500'. From there it rolls over small hills, with an optional steep climb to the top of Mt. Cushman, adding 1,000'.
Season: June through September are the best months for riding.
Services: All services are located in attractive Rochester, including a bike shop, American Youth Hostel lodge (for all ages), a good bed-and-breakfast inn managed by mountain bikers, and inexpensive restaurants.
Hazards: Watch out for traffic on VT 100. Most motorists, fortunately, have become used to cyclists on this most scenic highway in Vermont.
Rescue index: There are many homes scattered along the way, and some well traveled roads nearby.
Land status: Active county and state roads.
Maps: A detailed state map will do or *The Vermont Atlas and Gazetteer* (DeLorme Mapping Co.), available in many stores. A Green Mountain National Forest office on VT 100 in Rochester sells USGS maps. The Green Mountain Bicycle Service in Rochester displays a wall of topographical maps.
Finding the trail: Begin the ride in Rochester on VT 100. (See "Notes on the trail.")

Sources of additional information:

> Green Mountain National Forest Office
> Rochester Ranger District
> VT 100, RD 1, Box 108
> Rochester, Vermont 05767
> (802) 767-4777

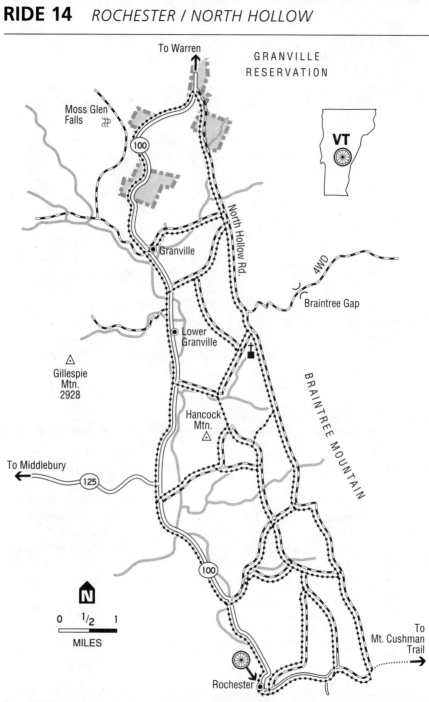

To Warren

GRANVILLE
RESERVATION

Moss Glen
Falls

100

VT

Granville

North Hollow Rd.

4WD

Braintree Gap

Lower
Granville

Gillespie
Mtn.
2928

Hancock
Mtn.

B R A I N T R E E   M O U N T A I N

To Middlebury

125

100

N

0   1/2   1

MILES

To
Mt. Cushman
Trail

Rochester

Green Mountain Bicycle Service
P.O. Box 253
Rochester, Vermont 05767
(802) 767-4464

Located in the center of quaint Rochester, on VT 100, this small business rents, repairs, and sells mountain bikes. It also specializes in guiding individuals and groups on leisurely, or more challenging, excursions. Stop in for a visit.

The Huntington House Inn on the Green in Rochester, (802) 767-4868, is owned by a mountain biker.

Notes on the trail: You can climb fairly steeply to North Hollow Road on Bethel Mountain Road and Brook Street, beginning at the Green in Rochester. A less steep climb begins on a dirt road 1.5 miles north of Rochester on VT 100. Turn right just after a large house and barn and before a bridge. After a half mile, fork to the right, then right again at the next fork (although either road leads to North Hollow Road). When you reach North Hollow Road, go in either direction (north or south) depending on how far you want to ride. Whatever loop you choose, a mountain range to the east and VT 100 to the west will keep you from straying too far. For a day-long excursion, ride north to Granville. Otherwise, simply turn west at a crossroad and descend to VT 100.

For the more adventurous, there's an optional out-and-back ride up a mountain. Just east of Rochester, turn off North Hollow Road at an abandoned house onto a road that leads eastward to Mt. Cushman. Ask at the local bike shop about this and other rides in the area.

RIDE 15 *MAD RIVER*

This 25-mile tour will test your climbing ability. After about five miles you tackle a two-mile climb on a two-wheel-drive dirt road, followed immediately by a two-mile descent. The rest of the ride is a rolling tour on dirt roads, a few miles of pavement, and a stretch on a four-wheel-drive jeep road. There's plenty of classic Vermont scenery along the way: large farms, a lively river, a horse farm, rural homes, a small town, and mountains on the horizon. There's also a swimming spot in the Mad River on the last stretch of the ride.

This area, known for Sugarbush—the popular ski resort in Waitsfield—has several cross-country ski areas that now allow mountain biking on groomed trails. Also, along VT 100 you can browse in antique shops, eateries, restaurants, sports shops, and art galleries.

General location: East of Waitsfield off VT 100.
Elevation change: Except for a steep 2-mile ascent, followed by a steep descent,

RIDE 15 *MAD RIVER*

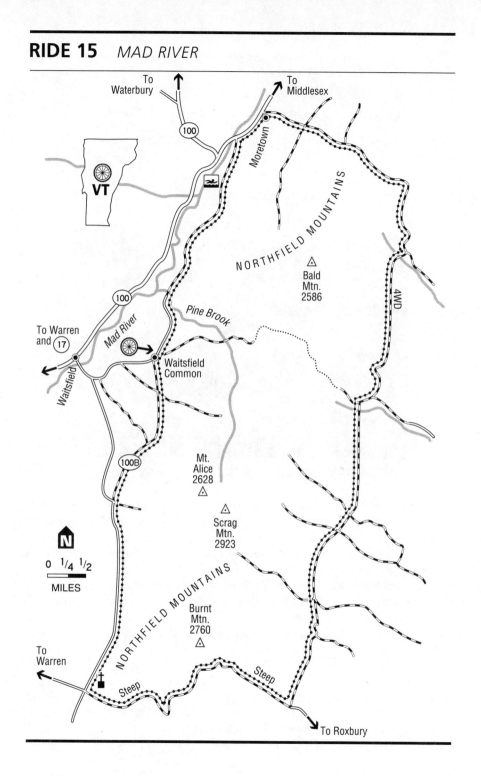

Rolling through open countryside. Waitsfield, Vermont.

the ride is on rolling terrain with a few climbs. This ride begins at 1,073', climbs to 2,300', descends steeply and then gradually to 602', and climbs back to 1,073'. Total elevation change is 1,700'.

Season: There is good riding between mid-June and fall. Expect muddy roads in the spring.

Services: All services are available in Waitsfield, Moretown, Warren, and along VT 100, including Mad River Bike Shop on Route 100 in Waitsfield, just south of the junction with VT 17.

Hazards: A steep, winding descent on an active dirt road demands concentration and good braking.

Rescue index: You are never far from civilization.

Land status: Town roads.

Maps: Any detailed state map will do, or pick up *The Vermont Atlas and Gazetteer.* It is available in many stores, or from the DeLorme Mapping Co., Box 298, Freeport, Maine, 04032. Phone: (207) 865-4171.

Finding the trail: On VT 100, 1 mile north of the junction with VT 17 in Waitsfield, turn right, pass a covered bridge, fork left, and climb. After about a mile you will reach a cemetery on the left in Waitsfield Common. Park along the cemetery.

Sources of additional information: The Mad River Bike Shop on Route 100 in Waitsfield, at the junction of VT 17, has plenty of information about mountain bike rides in this area. Phone: (802) 496-9500.

Notes on the trail: From Waitsfield Common ride south on a gravel road toward the sign "Greenhouse." Enjoy good views as you roll up and down, reaching pavement at 2.4 miles. Stay on the pavement for about 3 miles, passing a cemetery in an open field on the left, just before an intersection with a sign pointing to the left: "Roxbury Mountain."

Turn left and prepare to climb. The pavement becomes hard-packed dirt and you climb steeply for 1.5 miles. Then descend for 2 miles, reaching pavement again. At the bottom of the hill turn left onto the first dirt road, then left at a fork after about 1 mile, and at upcoming intersections make sure you keep heading north toward Moretown. After about 4 miles you reach a "T" junction. Turn right, then immediately left. After another mile, passing over a bridge, the road becomes a rugged jeep trail. After about 1.5 miles you will reach a broad, unpaved road. Turn left on it, and begin a long descent. Fork left after another 2.2 miles and continue descending into Moretown, coming out on VT 100.

Turn left, ride through town, and turn at the first road on the left with a sign: "Load Limit 24,000 lbs." After a short, steep climb you pass a river and swimming spot on the right. After 3 miles on this scenic road you'll go through a covered bridge. The road becomes paved for a short, steep climb, and you will arrive at Waitsfield Common.

RIDE 16   *ROXBURY STATE FOREST*

This ten-mile loop takes in a variety of riding conditions: a climb up a two-wheel-drive dirt road, level riding through a lightly wooded state forest on a grassy road for several miles, a half-mile descent on a rugged trail, and a cruise along a scenic paved road for three miles.

The mid-section of the ride cuts through a secluded state forest, passing light woods, a beaver pond, and wild berry bushes in the summer. The last three miles of the ride, on a scenic paved road, parallel a river, pass through a small town, and run by an old railroad and a fish and wildlife hatchery.

General location: Just outside Roxbury on VT 12A and 15 miles south of Montpelier.

Elevation change: You climb somewhat steeply for almost 2 miles (a 900' elevation gain), then cruise on a flat road for several miles and descend.

RIDE 16 *ROXBURY STATE FOREST*

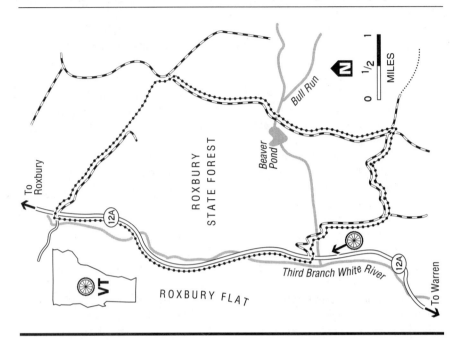

Season: Any time from mid-June through the fall is good riding.

Services: A country store in Roxbury has gas, food, and drink. All other services are available in Montpelier, 15 miles away.

Hazards: Watch for vehicles on the dirt roads while ascending and descending. Also, be prepared for the switch from a grassy road to a downhill stretch on a rugged trail.

Rescue index: You are never more than half a mile from assistance.

Land status: Town road and state forest roads.

Maps: A detailed state map will do, or pick up a collection of state maps— *The Vermont Atlas and Gazetteer* (DeLorme Mapping Co., Box 298, Freeport, Maine, 04032, (207) 865-4171)—available in many stores.

Finding the trail: There is a parking area on VT 12A 3 miles south of Roxbury.

Sources of additional information: Mad River Bike Shop on Route 100 in Waitsfield, at the junction of VT 17, has plenty of information about mountain bike rides in this area. Phone: (802) 496-9500.

Notes on the trail: From the parking lot on VT 12A ride north for two-tenths of a mile, and turn right up a dirt road marked "Legal Load Limit 24,000 lbs." Turn right at a fork and climb, forking left on the way. At two miles turn left at the first major dirt road intersection—you're now in the state forest. You will pass a beaver pond and clearing, and then a house and dirt road on the right.

Just opposite the road on the right, there's a grassy trail into the woods. It's a fun half-mile descent, with ruts, rocks, and some mud. (If you prefer to remain on dirt roads, continue on the state forest road for another mile, turn left at the only "T" intersection, and descend into Roxbury.) The trail comes out on a dirt road. Turn right on it, and descend for a mile into Roxbury. Turn left on VT 12A and return to the parking lot.

RIDE 17 *HUBBARD PARK*

In the midst of the handsome capital city of Montpelier is an elevated 100-acre park with about two and a half miles of quiet dirt roads. You'll probably want to make several loops through the park, enjoying the stands of hardwoods and open fields. The main gravel loop for biking is gated, to prohibit four-wheel vehicles from using it. This ride is a couple of miles from the Jones Brook ride.

Hubbard Park also has several picnic areas (which fill up on weekends), an aerobic fitness course, nature trails, and a ball-playing field. Montpelier is a lively and artistic center, with many festivals in the summer and fall, including an ice

RIDE 17 *HUBBARD PARK*

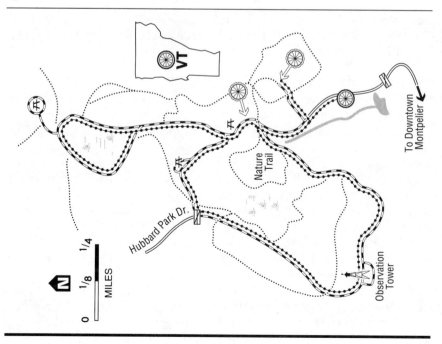

An unpaved road in Hubbard Park. Montpelier, Vermont.

cream festival in July and autumn festivals dedicated to apples and crafts. There's also a free museum of "Vermontiana," and you can tour the capitol, which has a dome covered with real gold.

General location: Montpelier.
Elevation change: If you begin in Montpelier it is a short, steep climb into the park. Otherwise, the roads in the park roll gently, with a few short climbs.
Season: You can ride here year-round. During the summer it's a pleasant, shady place.
Services: All services are available in Montpelier. Onion River Sports on Langdon Street, (802) 229-9409, will do immediate repairs for touring cyclists, and can suggest other rides. Also, ask them about bed-and-breakfast inns.
Hazards: None, but watch out for joggers, naturalists, and other park users.
Rescue index: The park is in a city, so you are never very far from people.
Land status: Town park roads.
Maps: A map is available from the Montpelier Recreation Department, (802) 223-5141. Onion River Sports has photocopies of it.
Finding the trail: Coming into Montpelier on VT 12, cross River Street, turn left on Spring Street (3 streets past the intersection of VT 12 and VT 2), and head up the steep Parkway. Turn left at the fork and enter Hubbard Park between 2

stone towers. There are parking areas along this access road and a larger one at the top of the hill.

Sources of additional information:

Hubbard Park Association
(802) 229-4319

Montpelier Recreation Department
(802) 223-5141

Onion River Sports
Langdon Street
Montpelier, Vermont 05602
(802) 229-9409

Notes on the trail: Biking is not allowed on the nature trails in the park.

RIDE 18 *JONES BROOK*

This ten-mile loop covers a lot of territory. It runs from the outskirts of Montpelier, along the wide Winooski River, through open countryside, into the woods, past a falls, and back to lively Montpelier through a landscape of fields, farms, and nodding wildflowers.

Fairly easy riding on hard-packed dirt roads at the beginning and on a scenic paved road at the end is broken up by a steep one-mile climb on a four-wheel-drive road. The ride can be connected with other loops to the west and south, and is a couple of miles from the Hubbard Park ride in Montpelier. (See that ride for a description of Montpelier.)

General location: Southwest of Montpelier.
Elevation change: The ride begins with a gradual climb, then a short, steep ascent, a steep descent, and a cruise back into Montpelier, for a total elevation change of 700′.
Season: Any time between mid-June and late autumn is good for riding.
Services: All services are available in Montpelier. Onion River Sports on Langdon Street, (802) 229-9409, does immediate repairs for touring cyclists and can suggest other rides. There's also a bed-and-breakfast in Montpelier run by a manager at Onion River Sports.
Hazards: Watch for oncoming traffic, especially when descending from the summit of the ride and along VT 12 heading back toward Montpelier.
Rescue index: You are never far from houses.
Land status: Town roads.
Maps: Any detailed state map will do, or pick up *The Vermont Atlas and Gazet-*

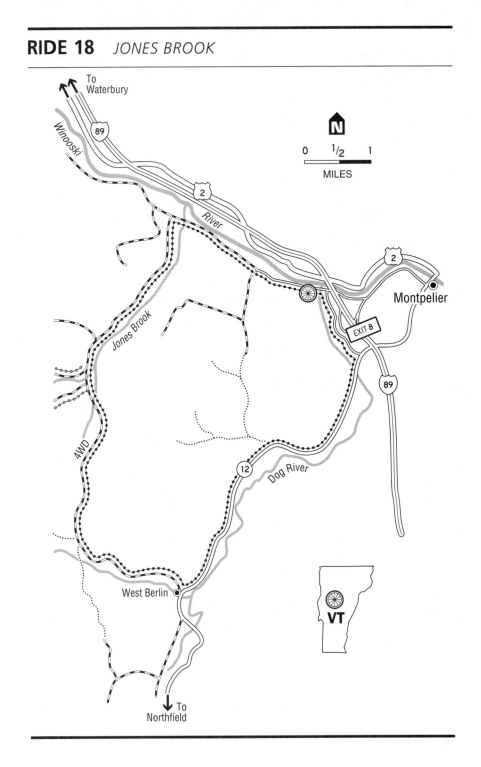

teer (DeLorme Mapping Co., Freeport, Maine), a collection of detailed road maps available in many stores.

Finding the trail: On Interstate 89 take Exit 8. While you're still on the exit ramp turn left at the sign for the railroad station. After about a half mile fork right across a narrow bridge, heading toward the railroad station. Travel one-third of a mile after the bridge and park in the large railroad parking lot on the left.

Sources of additional information:

Onion River Sports
Langdon Street
Montpelier, Vermont 05602
(802) 229-9409

Notes on the trail: Ride along the river for about 2 miles and turn left just after a large farm, onto a hard-packed dirt road with a sign reading "Jones Brook." Stay to the left (several steeper roads fork to the right). After 2 miles there's a sign for Herring Brook to the right. This is an optional loop. Otherwise, begin climbing, as the road becomes narrower, grassier, rockier, and steeper. Then descend along a brook with dramatic ledges. Next you will turn left at a stop sign at VT 12, and ride on the paved shoulder of this scenic road for about 4 miles. Before going uphill, just before a 1-story building on the left, turn left onto Dog River Road. After seven-tenths of a mile you will come out at the bridge before the railroad station. Turn left, cross the bridge, and reach the railroad parking lot.

RIDE 19 *WHEELOCK*

This nine-mile loop (with an optional seven-mile extension) explores the "real" Vermont: an uncommercialized landscape of fields, woods, modest houses, a church or two, brooks, and ponds. Along the way you'll even ride "through" a dairy farm, which crowds the narrow road on either side—as if no one was expected to come by. Most of the ride uses two-wheel-drive dirt roads, with two miles on a technical jeep trail.

General location: The ride passes through the towns of Wheelock and North Danville.

Elevation change: This is rolling terrain with some steady, not-too-steep climbing and a short, steeper climb and descent on a jeep trail.

Season: Riding is best between mid-June and fall. Expect mud in the spring.

Services: All services are available in Lyndon, 3 miles east on Interstate 91. In Lyndonville, the Village Sport Shop on Route 5, (802) 626-8448, is open for sales and service 7 days a week.

Hazards: Be prepared to switch from smooth two-wheel-drive roads to a jeep

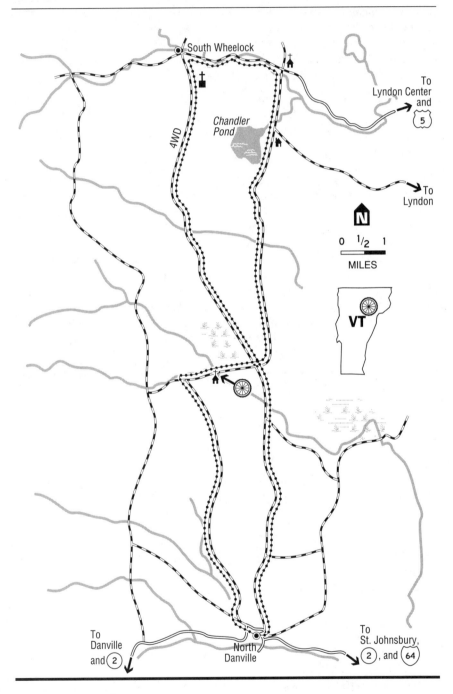

South Wheelock

To Lyndon Center and (5)

4WD

Chandler Pond

To Lyndon

N

0 1/2 1
MILES

VT

To Danville and (2)

North Danville

To St. Johnsbury, (2), and (64)

trail. When you pass "through" the dairy farm watch out for cows grazing next to the narrow, unfenced road. (The black-and-white cows are Holsteins, whose distinctive coloring has become a symbol for Vermont.)

Rescue index: You will regularly pass homes and cabins on this ride.

Land status: Active town roads.

Maps: A detailed state road map will do.

Finding the trail: Take Exit 21 off Interstate 91, onto VT 2 heading west. After a couple of miles, turn right toward North Danville. In North Danville, turn left at a fork just before a white church on the far left corner. After 1.2 miles, turn right onto a dirt road, toward a sign "Old North Church." After 2.7 miles, turn right and reach the Old North Church on the right. Park behind the church.

Sources of additional information: The Village Sport Shop on Route 5 in Lyndonville, (802) 626-8448, is open 7 days a week.

Notes on the trail: Ride east from the Old North Church for eight-tenths of a mile until you reach an intersection. Turn left onto a narrower road, which becomes a jeep trail after about 1 mile. After about a half mile, fork left on this trail. The trail turns back into a two-wheel-drive road and comes out at an intersection with a bridge. Turn right and in a mile you will reach an intersection with a church on the left. Turn right, stay right at a fork after about a half mile, and after 2.7 miles you will reach the same intersection where you turned left before. Go straight to return to the Old North Church.

To extend this ride another 7 miles, turn left at the final intersection instead of going straight. After about 3 miles you reach a sharp, steep, paved right turn into North Danville. Veer right, pass over a bridge and through the town, taking a right fork at the white church on the far left corner (see "Finding the trail"). After a few hundred feet, turn right at a smaller dirt road with the sign, "Old North Church." This scenic, relatively flat road comes out at the Old North Church after 2.6 miles.

RIDE 20 *ELMORE MOUNTAIN ROAD*

This 12-mile loop climbs on a dirt road to a ridge with excellent views of the Stowe countryside: active farms and fields in the foreground and mountains looming just behind them. It is not a technical ride, but there is a fair amount of climbing on two-wheel-drive dirt roads—and a fun descent on dirt and pavement.

The Stowe area has been chosen for a "pilot" program to develop networks of mountain bike routes in Vermont. Drop by a local bike shop to find out where other mountain bike rides are in this recreation-oriented region, which also has opportunities for road riding, hiking, camping, fishing, and swimming. Ben and

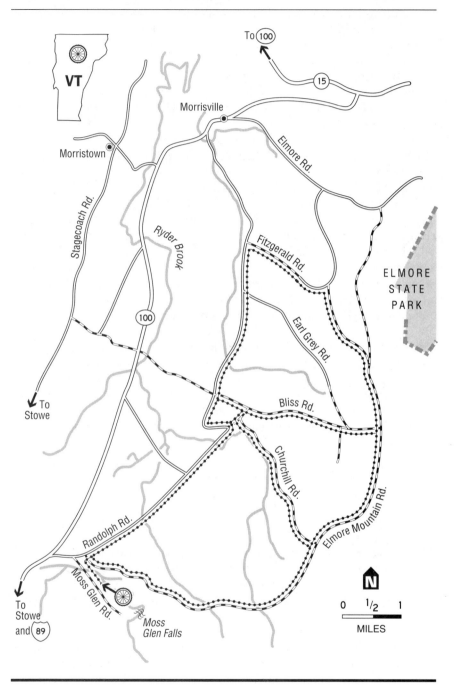

Jerry's gourmet ice cream factory is located in nearby Waterbury; there's a cider mill down the road that you can visit; and the famous Trapp Family Resort is nearby with its gift shop, restaurants, and concerts.

General location: Northeast of Stowe.

Elevation change: The ride is a steady, not-too-steep climb for about 4.5 miles and then a descent.

Season: Any time between mid-June and fall is fine.

Services: All services are available in Stowe, including three bike shops: Mountain Bike Shop, (802) 253-7919; Stowe Action Outfitter, (802) 253-7975; and Stowe Mountain Sports, (802) 253-5896.

Hazards: None except for occasional light traffic.

Rescue index: You are always near houses.

Land status: Town roads.

Maps: Lamoille County, where Stowe is located, has produced a brown map, "Summer Recreation Map & Guide for the Mt. Mansfield Region," which lists a dozen mountain bike rides (as well as other recreational information). A good collection of detailed maps is *The Vermont Atlas and Gazetteer* (DeLorme Mapping Co., Freeport, Maine), available in many stores.

Finding the trail: Take Exit 10 off Interstate 89, and head 10 miles north on VT 100 into Stowe. Continue past the junction with VT 108, then fork right onto Randolph Road after another 2.8 miles. After one-third mile, turn right onto Moss Glen Road. In another half mile you will reach a parking area (for Moss Glen Falls).

Sources of additional information: Contact the Mountain Bike Shop on Mountain Road (VT 108) in Stowe, Vermont, (802) 253-7919. This shop specializes in mountain biking, and offers rentals, maps, advice, and guided tours.

Notes on the trail: Ride back up Moss Glen Road, turn right, and right again onto Elmore Mountain Road. You will climb gently, then more steeply. Take time to appreciate the views. After about 3 miles you will pass a dirt road on the left—Churchhill Road. You can take this road back to Randolph Road for a shorter loop. There's a grand view on the left, then an active farm on either side of the road. A left turn on a dirt road near the farm house, Bliss Road, also comes out on Randolph Road.

After about another mile on Elmore Mountain Road, at the top of a short hill, there's a soft left fork onto unmarked Mountain Road. Turn there and go downhill for a mile, until you reach pavement. Fork left onto Fitzgerald Road. After a mile you will reach a stop sign at Randolph Road. Turn left and ride for 4.5 miles back to Moss Glen Road.

RIDE 21 *MUD CITY*

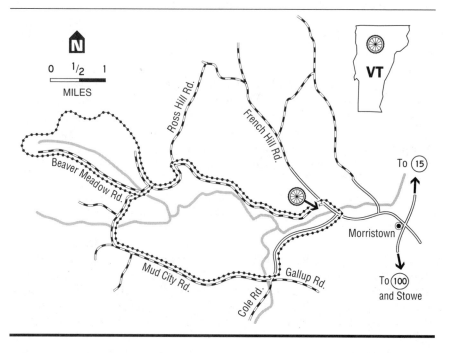

RIDE 21 *MUD CITY*

This ten-mile ride traces a figure-eight shape—or two interconnecting loops. The larger loop is made up of six miles of two-wheel-drive dirt roads through scenic, inhabited countryside; the smaller loop has 2.5 miles of riding on secluded trails and 1.5 miles on dirt roads. Despite its locally designated name, there is little mud on this ride.

You can do either loop separately (see map and "Notes on the trail"). When ridden as a figure-eight, however, the route offers the stimulation of smooth dirt roads with panoramic views, moderately technical riding in intimate deep woods, and then more cruising through the scenic landscape.

General location: Morristown, 8 miles north of Stowe.
Elevation change: The first half of the ride is a steady, occasionally steep climb on roads and trails; not surprisingly, the second half goes steadily downhill.
Season: Mid-June through fall offers good riding.
Services: All services are available in Stowe, including 3 bike shops: Mountain

Bike Shop, (802) 253-7919; Stowe Action Outfitter, (802) 253-7975; and Stowe Mountain Sports, (802) 253-5896.

Hazards: Watch out for traffic on the two-wheel-drive roads. There may be some minor obstructions on the trails, especially in late summer and fall when they become overgrown.

Rescue index: You are never more than a mile from a traveled road.

Land status: Active town roads and an abandoned town road.

Maps: Lamoille County, where Stowe is located, has produced a brown map, "Summer Recreation Map & Guide for the Mt. Mansfield Region," which lists a dozen mountain bike rides (as well as other recreational information). A good collection of detailed maps is *The Vermont Atlas and Gazetteer* (DeLorme Mapping Co., Freeport, Maine), available in many stores.

Finding the trail: Take Exit 10 on Interstate 89, heading 10 miles north on VT 100. Continue past the junction with VT 108 in Stowe, and after 1.5 miles, fork left onto Stagecoach Road. After another 5.5 miles you will reach an intersection with a country store and houses. Turn left then veer left after two-tenths of a mile; fork right at six-tenths of a mile. Go over a bridge, and fork left at eight-tenths of a mile. Park off the road on the right.

Sources of additional information: The Mountain Bike Shop on Mountain Road (VT 108) in Stowe, Vermont, (802) 253-7919, specializes in mountain biking, including rentals, maps, advice, and guided tours.

Notes on the trail: Ride steadily up the road past fields and woods. After 1.7 miles, turn left at a "T" junction. After another half mile you will pass a road on the right, where the smaller loop comes out. After another three-tenths of a mile, at a large farm on the left, turn right up Beaver Meadow Road. In a mile you will reach a clearing on the right, before the road becomes a jeep trail into the woods. (You can begin a shorter, more technical ride here on a 4-mile loop with 2.5 miles of trail riding.)

Head up into the woods, and immediately after crossing a stream at seven-tenths of a mile, fork right on a narrower trail, which may have an orange diamond snowmobile marker on it. After another 1.5 miles, turn left on a gravel road as you pass a pond on the right. When you've traveled another half mile or so, you will come out on the same gravel road that you pedaled up before. Turn right, ride past the farm, and now go straight while watching out for oncoming vehicles. After about 2 miles you will reach a stop sign at a paved road. Turn left, and in a mile, you'll reach another stop sign. Turn left sharply, pass over a bridge, and turn left again to complete the figure-eight.

RIDE 22 *BOLTON VALLEY*

This resort has 62 miles of interconnecting trails, from easy, shorter loops to steeper, more technical ones. They're all open for riding from late spring through fall. At 3,000 feet above sea level, this may be the highest trail riding in all of Vermont. About a third of the resort's double-track trails are groomed, while the rest are more rugged. One main trail, Broadway, is a wide, smooth road.

If you've never visited nearby Burlington, it's worth it. The city has a paved bikepath along scenic Lake Champlain, several bike shops, good restaurants, and the campus of the University of Vermont.

General location: Four miles north of Bolton.
Elevation change: Trails vary from the beginner level to steeper, advanced routes. Total elevation change is from 1,600' to about 3,000'.
Season: Because of its elevation (2,100') the resort opens for biking somewhat later in the spring than do places at lower altitudes. It also closes slightly earlier in the fall. Call ahead in these seasons: (800) 451-3220.
Services: All services are available at the ski resort (at slightly higher prices) or along US 2. There's a rustic cabin on the mountain that you can reserve overnight.
Hazards: Watch for minor obstructions along these ski trails. Make sure your brakes are in good shape before tackling steeper trails.
Rescue index: You will be only a couple of miles from assistance at any time.
Land status: Private resort trails.
Maps: Trail maps are available at the Touring Center at the base lodge and at the resort's main information desk.
Finding the trail: From Interstate 89 take Exit 11 for Richmond and Bolton. Head east on US 2 for 7.9 miles. The access road to Bolton Valley Ski Area is on the left, immediately after you pass under I-89. Head up the access road for 4 miles and park at the resort.

Sources of additional information:

Bolton Valley Resort
Bolton, Vermont 05477
(800) 451-3220

Ski Rack
85 Main Street
Burlington, Vermont 05401
(802) 658-3313

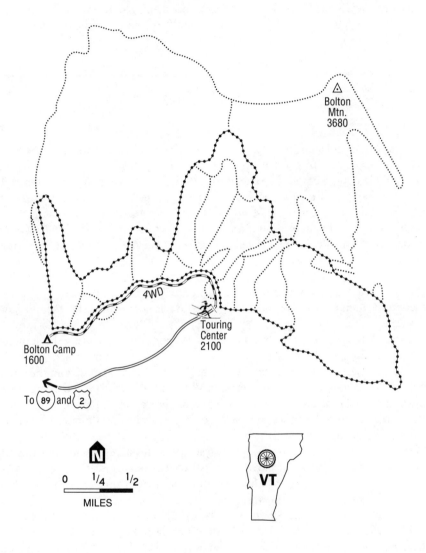

Bolton
Mtn.
3680

4WD

Touring
Center
2100

Bolton Camp
1600

To (89) and (2)

N

0   1/4   1/2

MILES

VT

North Star Cyclery
100 Main Street
Burlington, Vermont 05401
(802) 863-3832

Notes on the trail: For less technical riding, take the four-wheel-drive dirt road (actually a wide trail) Broadway, that forks off the paved access road to the left as you drive up the mountain. It begins at 1,600′ and climbs to the touring center at 2,100′. Many other trails fork off Broadway.

RIDE 23 *CATAMOUNT CENTER*

You can construct shorter or longer rides on the 20 miles of trails at this cross-country ski center. In general, the farther you ride from the parking lot, the more challenging the trails become. For starters there's a six-mile perimeter trail. Most of the trails are manageable by a novice, yet technical enough to keep an experienced rider entertained. A bike shop in Burlington holds races here.

Unlike most mountain biking areas, this one offers a lot of riding in open fields. You then enter the pine-filled woods and come out again, catching a view of mountains on the horizon.

General location: Eight miles east of Burlington, off US 2.
Elevation change: This is relatively flat terrain with occasional short climbs and descents.
Season: Any time between June and late fall is good riding. During the summer the woods offer shade while the open fields provide warmth in cooler weather.
Services: There is a restroom and water behind the house across from the parking lot. All other services are available in Williston, Burlington, and along US 2. Burlington is an attractive city. It is home of the campus of the University of Vermont, several bike shops, a hostel, good restaurants, and a paved bikepath along Lake Champlain.
Hazards: Wetness can cause slickness on steeper sections, especially on protruding tree roots. A map at the parking lot lists other safety tips.
Rescue index: You will be about a mile from help on accessible terrain. Traveled roads surround the area.
Land status: Private cross-country ski trails. Note: There's a box at the parking lot where you're asked to pay $3.00 on an honor system.
Maps: Maps are usually stocked at the parking lot. Trail lengths are given in kilometers (1 km=.62 miles). Many trails are marked at intersections.
Finding the trail: Take Exit 12 on Interstate 89 (about 5 miles east of Burlington) toward Williston and 2A. Turn north on VT 2A and east on US 2. After

RIDE 23 *CATAMOUNT CENTER*

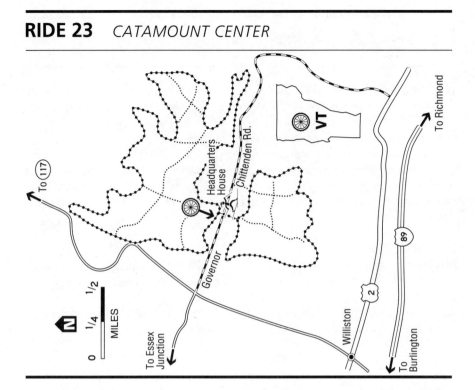

2 miles turn north onto North Williston Road for 1 mile, then east on Governor Chittenden Road. After a mile you will reach the parking lot at the Catamount Center on the left.

Sources of additional information:

Catamount Center
421 Governor Chittenden Road
Williston, Vermont 05495
(802) 879-6001

Ski Rack
85 Main Street
Burlington, Vermont 05401
(802) 658-3313

Notes on the trail: At first, this network of trails can seem confusing, but notice that they're built up in concentric circles and you won't have any difficulty deciphering them.

RIDE 24   *CRAFTSBURY RIDGE*

This ten-mile loop gives you a taste of riding in the Northeast Kingdom, a region in upstate Vermont known for its unspoiled, lightly inhabited landscape. The ride, which rolls over hard-packed dirt roads, is surrounded by about 200 miles of other scenic dirt roads, including the Albany ride.

After climbing gently for a couple of miles, you will reach excellent views of the surrounding landscape: small towns, tidy farms, rolling fields, and large ponds. These sights are highlighted by ever-changing wooded mountains. Delicate spring hues change to deep summer greens, brilliant fall colors, and stark winter whites.

General location: Craftsbury.
Elevation change: This rolling terrain has regular, gentle climbs and descents.
Season: June through late autumn is good riding. Expect mud on the roads in early spring.
Services: All services are available in Craftsbury and at the Craftsbury Center, an overnight sports center near Craftsbury Common.

Cruising in the secluded Northeast Kingdom. Craftsbury, Vermont.

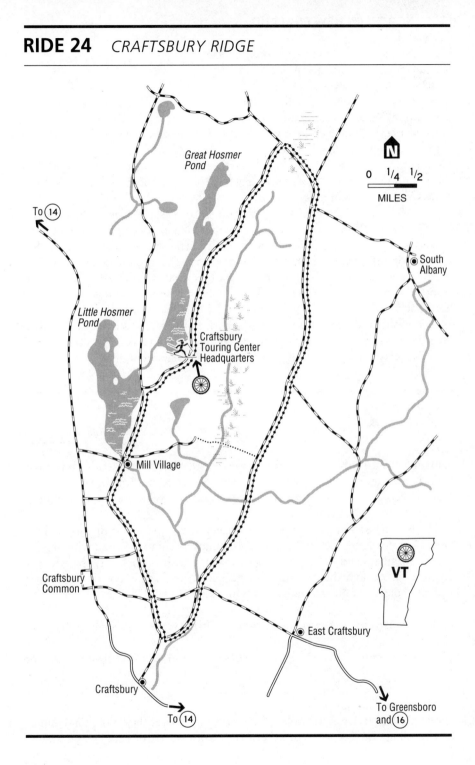

Hazards: None except for occasional vehicles.

Rescue index: You are always near houses.

Land status: Town roads.

Maps: The Craftsbury Center in Craftsbury Common has maps and written descriptions of many mountain bike rides in the area. *The Vermont Atlas and Gazetteer* (DeLorme Mapping Co., Freeport, Maine), a detailed book of state maps, is available in many stores.

Finding the trail: On VT 14, 2 miles northeast of Craftsbury Common, follow the white signs for the "Craftsbury Center." You can park in their parking lot.

Sources of additional information: Known for years as a mecca for cross-country skiers, the Craftsbury Center (Box 31, Craftsbury Common, Vermont, 05827, (800) 729-7751) now serves mountain bikers, also. Located in a region of Vermont known for its beauty and relative lack of tourism, the Center has a mountain bike center offering rentals, maps, repairs, group rides, instruction, use of a ski trails system, and a mountain bike festival in the fall. This rustic resort also has lodging, meals, parking, and other sports such as boating and horseback riding.

Notes on the trail: Ride north from the parking lot on the dirt road, and make right turns at all intersections until you complete a loop. You can do a mirror-image ride, too, by making all left turns, circling a large pond.

RIDE 25 *ALBANY*

This moderate 15-mile ride explores some of the scenic dirt roads and grassy trails in this more secluded part of Vermont known as the Northeast Kingdom. The loop connects with many more miles of scenic roads and trails, including the Craftsbury Ridge ride.

The Northeast Kingdom is popular because it has preserved the original flavor of Vermont: tidy farms, rolling fields, ponds, small towns, and white-spired churches, all framed by distant mountains and nearby woods. Its palette also changes throughout the year: delicate hues in spring, shady greens in summer, brilliant colors in fall, and quiet whites in winter.

General location: The ride passes from Craftsbury into the neighboring town of Albany.

Elevation change: This rolling terrain has about 150′ of climbing on roads and trails.

Season: Any time between mid-June and fall offers good riding. Expect mud on roads and trails in spring.

Services: All services are available in Craftsbury and at the Craftsbury Center, an overnight outdoor recreational center in Craftsbury Common.

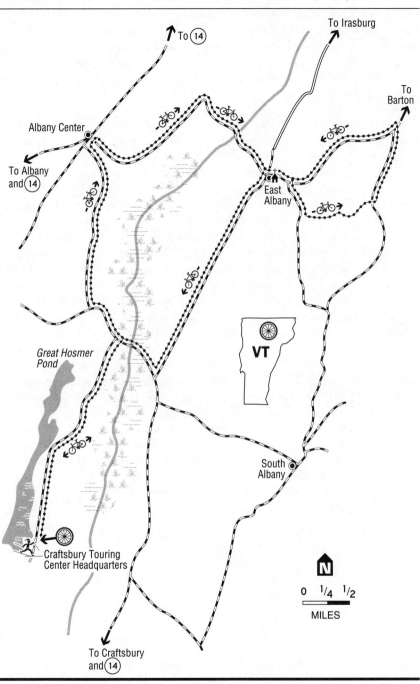

To (14)

To Irasburg

To
Barton

Albany Center

To Albany
and (14)

East
Albany

VT

Great Hosmer
Pond

South
Albany

Craftsbury Touring
Center Headquarters

N

0   1/4   1/2

MILES

To Craftsbury
and (14)

Hazards: At two sites along this ride you must stoop under a marked, waist-high electric fence (designed to keep farm animals from straying). Be careful.

Rescue index: You will never be far from houses or cabins.

Land status: Active and abandoned town roads.

Maps: The Craftsbury Center in Craftsbury Common has maps of mountain bike rides, available for a small charge. *The Vermont Atlas and Gazetteer* (DeLorme Mapping Co., Freeport, Maine) is available at many stores in Vermont.

Finding the trail: Turn off VT 14 about 2 miles northeast of Craftsbury Common, and follow the white signs for "Craftsbury Center." Park in the center's parking lot.

Sources of additional information: Craftsbury Center, Box 31, Craftsbury Common, Vermont, 05827, (800) 729-7751. This 17-year-old center now offers guided and self-guided mountain bike tours, maps, a bike repair shop, lodging and meals, and a mountain bike festival each fall.

Notes on the trail: Head north from the parking lot at the Craftsbury Center on a hard-packed dirt road for a couple of miles. Turn left at the "T" junction, heading uphill. After about a half mile, turn right going downhill. After a mile when the road turns right, head straight on a four-wheel-drive trail into the woods. In another mile veer left, then right, coming out in Albany Center. After some 100 yards, just before a large house, turn right onto another dirt road. In about a mile veer to the left while staying on the road, then to the right. Go downhill; you'll reach an electric fence in front of a field. Although this looks like private land, it is a public road. At the intersection with a church on the far right corner, head straight toward Barton. Veer right at the first fork, then left after one-third mile, passing over a brook on a wooden bridge. Veer to the right up what looks like a streambed; it becomes a grassy, single-track path.

You will reach an electric horse fence and then an intersection. Turn left, and after about a mile take a sharp left. This road will come out at the intersection with the church (now on the left). Turn left and ride along good views for about 2 miles. Turn right at the first junction, and after another half mile ride left uphill. You're now on the road that passes the Craftsbury Center.

NEW HAMPSHIRE

RIDE 26 GREENVILLE RAIL TRAIL

A "rail trail" is a former railroad bed with its ties removed, making it a smooth, ultraflat cinder path. This one runs through light woods and rural countryside for six and a half miles, from a small town in New Hampshire to the border of Massachusetts. You can do a contemplative ride along this historical corridor, where steam engines once ran, or crank along at 15 miles per hour.

General location: Just outside Greenville and Mason.
Elevation change: Flat, Railroad beds were designed to rise no more than two degrees from level.
Season: Any time between mid-June and fall is good for riding.
Services: All services are available in Greenville.
Hazards: Watch out for an occasional all-terrain vehicle on this trail—although they are prohibited. Depending on the amount of moisture, mosquitoes can arrive in late spring and early summer.
Rescue index: You are never more than a mile from traveled roads.
Land status: As a sign near its southern end tells you, this trail is a cooperative recreational project of the U.S. National Park Service, the state of New Hampshire, and abutting towns.
Maps: *The New Hampshire Atlas and Gazetteer* (DeLorme Mapping Co., Freeport, Maine, 04032), a collection of non-topographical maps of all byways in the state, is available at many stores.
Finding the trail: Two miles north of the junction of NH 31 and NH 123, you pass giant trestles on both sides of the highway. They are the remnants of a railroad bridge. Turn right past these nineteenth-century ruins onto steep Adams Hill Road. After a few hundred feet there is a small parking area on the right. The trail goes to the left.

You can begin riding at the original depot in Greenville (now a restaurant), but after a half mile you'll encounter an impassable gulch that the railroad bridge once spanned. To continue, you must get onto a road on the right that parallels the trail before reaching the gulch. Head out of Greenville turning left on NH 31, then right onto Adams Hill Road.

There's a southern trailhead at a small parking lot on Depot Road in Mason, 5 miles south of Greenville and a half mile west of Townsend Road.
Sources of additional information: The Rails-to-Trails Conservancy (1400 16th St., NW, Washington, D.C., 20036, (202) 797-5400) is a national clearinghouse for rail trails throughout the country. Several rides in this book, especially in New Hampshire and Maine, are rail trails—old railroad beds from which the ties have been removed. New Hampshire was once known as the Railroad State. As more railroads are abandoned, rail trails are being created throughout the

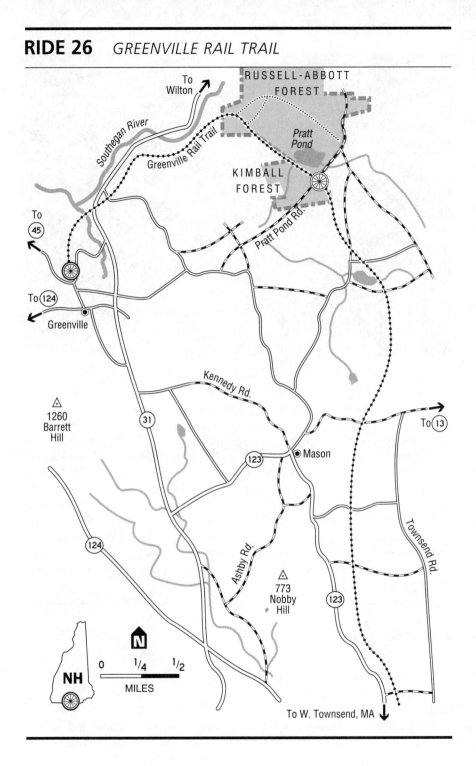

A former railroad bed—now a smooth, scenic trail. Greenville, New Hampshire.

United States. They are sponsored by many local outdoor enthusiasts: walkers, bicyclists, motorized bikers, equestrians, and skiers.

Notes on the trail: You can ride on this trail all the way to the Massachusetts border, a 6.5-mile trip. (Then it reverts to tracks and ties with thick underbrush on either side.) You can also do an optional 5-mile loop with some climbing on dirt and paved roads. While heading south, a few hundred yards before the Massachusetts border, you'll reach Morse Road, a two-wheel-drive dirt road with a small waterfall on the left. Turn left and after less than a mile you reach Townsend Road. Turn left onto paved Townsend Road, and after about 2 miles through scenic countryside turn left again on Depot Road. Go downhill until you cross the rail trail after about a half mile. Turn right and head back north.

RIDE 27 *POTANIPO HILL*

This seven-mile loop takes you to a panoramic view from the top of a mountain, as well as through pleasant woods and lightly inhabited countryside. The ride begins with the classic rural scene: people fishing from a bridge and swimming in ponds. But you're looking for good mountain biking, so it's up and into the woods. After climbing gently for about a mile, you will arrive at a sweeping view

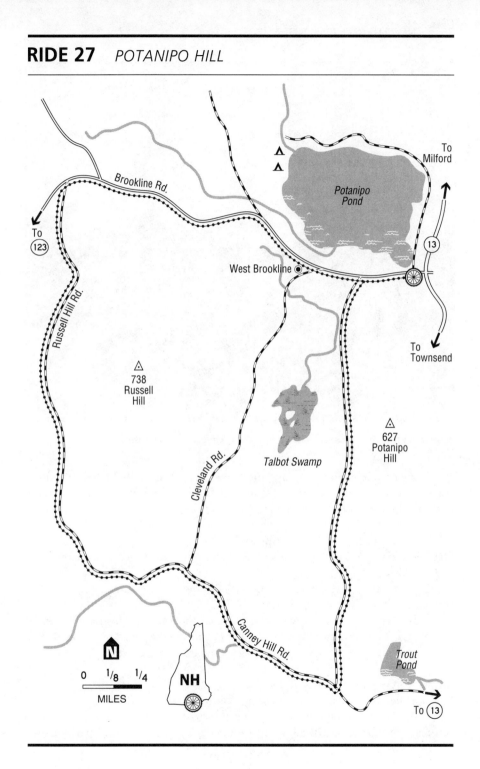

To Milford

Potanipo Pond

To 123

Brookline Rd.

West Brookline

13

Russell Hill Rd.

To Townsend

⚠
738
Russell
Hill

Cleveland Rd.

⚠
627
Potanipo
Hill

Talbot Swamp

N

0   1/8   1/4
MILES

NH

Carney Hill Rd.

Trout
Pond

To 13

Bird-watching at the peak. Potanipo Hill, Brookline, New Hampshire.

from a surprisingly modest mountain (491'). The ride uses double-track trails, a gravel road, two scenic paved roads, and a four-wheel-drive dirt road. According to locals there is good bird-watching along this loop.

General location: In the town of Brookline, off NH 13.
Elevation change: This ride gains a total of 900' in a series of fairly short climbs and descents.
Season: Any time between mid-June and fall is good for riding.
Services: All services are available on NH 13.
Hazards: Watch for occasional mud holes in the woods. Mosquitoes can be prevalent in early summer. And there is light traffic on the paved Brookline Road.
Rescue index: You are never more than a mile from assistance.
Land status: Town roads.
Maps: USGS, Townsend, MA, NH.
Finding the trail: From the Massachusetts border, take NH 13 north for 2.5 miles. At a blinking light with a sign on the right ("Meeting House Hill Rd.") turn left onto Brookline Road. Turn left immediately into a sunken parking area

next to a stream and bridge. To reach the trailhead ride west on Brookline Road, cross the bridge, pass several homes, and turn left up an unpaved road. The road climbs past a large house and tennis court on the left and enters the woods.

Sources of additional information: Ask at the trailhead about this route.

Notes on the trail: Ride up and over the panoramic summit on a double-track trail. Descend and come out on paved Canney Hill Road. Turn right, stay to the right, and after 1 mile take a left fork onto a gravel road. Then fork to the right, and you will come to a fork with a trail straight ahead and a new road to the left. Take the trail into the woods. It becomes unpaved Russell Hill Road and descends to Brookline Road. Turn right, and ride for about 1.5 miles back to the parking area.

RIDE 28 *BEAVER BROOK WILDLIFE HABITAT*

You can ride for miles on the "woods roads" in this privately maintained wildlife habitat. Note: *Biking is not allowed on the trails.* This habitat is currently being reviewed for trail access policies. Cycling on the trails will lead to the banning of bikes.

As elsewhere in New England, you will encounter stone walls in these woods. Why did European settlers build so many walls? Most of the land in New England was once cleared and cultivated. Stone walls accomplished two tasks: getting rid of stones and creating boundaries. Then these settlers discovered the rockless Midwest. Stone walls are all that is left of those hard-working times.

The habitat is also a place for studying the stages of a New England forest. The process, known as "field succession," begins with small plants like lambsquarter and ragweed. Then larger flora—milkweed, thistle, and yarrow—take over. After about five years, small trees such as sumac, juniper, and hemlock dominate. Next, birches, aspen, and ashes take over. Finally, after about 40 years, a mature, stable forest develops, dominated by large maples, beeches, and white pines—if a fire doesn't start the whole process over once again. You can study this process at the habitat's educational centers or just ride through and enjoy it. Look for clearings, ponds, stands of hardwood and white pine trees, an apple orchard, and wildlife like cottontail rabbits, skunks, and woodpeckers.

General location: The town of Hollis on NH 122.

Elevation change: This ride is on relatively flat terrain with regular short climbs and descents.

Season: Any time between June and fall offers good riding conditions.

Services: Drinking water is available at the trailheads. All other services are available along NH 122 and in Hollis. And if you're in need of a bike shop, try

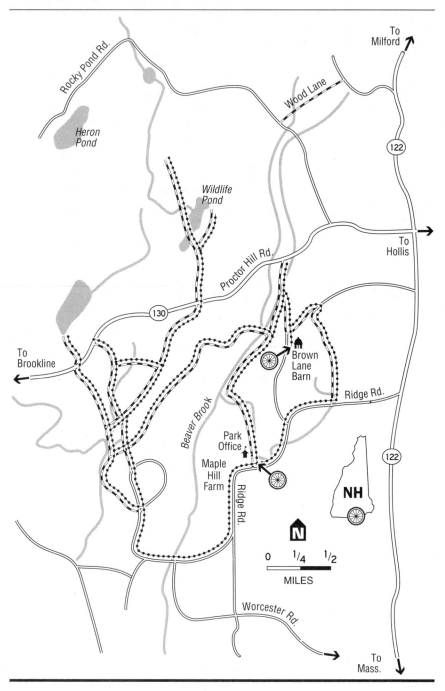

Goodale's Bike & Ski Shop, 46 Main Street, Nashua, New Hampshire, (603) 882-2111.

Hazards: None except the usual minor natural obstructions on some of the trails.

Rescue index: You are never more than half a mile from assistance.

Land status: This nature center allows biking on its "woods roads," many of which are double-track trails. The roads are also used by hikers, naturalists, equestrians, and families.

Maps: A map is available (for a nominal charge) at the 2 formal trailheads: Maple Hill Farm office and Brown Lane Barn, 117 Ridge Rd., (603) 465-7787. The office is open weekdays, 8:30–2:30. The trails are open 7 days a week until dark. Do not ride on designated nature trails.

Finding the trail: Take Exit 6 on US 3 in Nashua (just 35 miles north of Boston). Head west on NH 130 toward Hollis and Silver Lake State Park. After 5.5 miles you will reach the junction of NH 122 and NH 130. Turn left (south) onto NH 122. After 1 mile you pass a cemetery on the right, turn right onto Ridge Road. Soon you will reach a fork; either way leads to a trailhead. Straight ahead is the Maple Hill Farm office, while to the right is the Brown Lane Barn.

Sources of additional information:

Beaver Brook Association
117 Ridge Road
Hollis, New Hampshire 03049
(603) 465-7787

Notes on the trail: Pick up a map of the habitat at the trailheads, since not all the roads link up with each other.

RIDE 29 *HOLLIS TOWN FOREST*

This small forest has a network of about eight miles of double- and single-track trails. You can do a five-and-a-half-mile perimeter loop on double-track trails, or crisscross through the woods on more challenging single-track trails. Expect some wet areas and obstructions on these minimally maintained trails. And watch for the occasional hiker.

Just across from the forest there is swimming and picnicking at Silver Lake State Park (two-dollar admission charge). A quarter mile farther along NH 122 you can sample local apple-filled foods at a large orchard and store. This ride is two miles north of the Beaver Brook Wildlife Habitat ride.

General location: Town of Hollis.
Elevation change: This is relatively flat terrain with small hills.

RIDE 29 *HOLLIS TOWN FOREST*

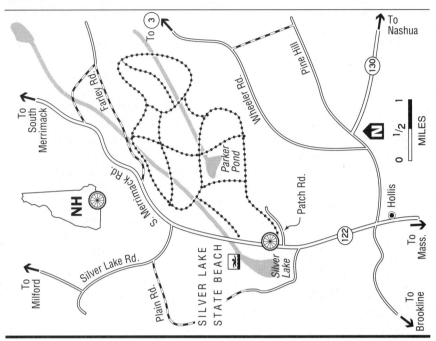

Season: Any time between mid-June and fall is good riding.

Services: There is water at the state park. All other services are available in Hollis and along NH 122. A bike shop is in nearby Nashua—Goodale's Bike and Ski Shop, (603) 882-2111.

Hazards: Watch out for occasional hikers and equestrians. Expect some mosquitoes in late spring and early summer.

Rescue index: You will be about a half mile from homes and traveled roads.

Land status: Town forest trails.

Maps: There is no official map of this forest. It is, however, compact and bounded by paved roads.

Finding the trail: Take Exit 6 on U.S. 3 in Nashua (35 miles north of Boston). Head west of NH 130 towards Hollis and Silver Lake State Park. After about 5 miles you will reach the junction of NH 130 and NH 122. Turn right on NH 122, following signs for Silver Lake State Park. After 1.2 miles you reach a large gravel parking lot on the right, across from the beach. To get to the trailhead, ride back down NH 122 to the first left turn, Patch Road. Take this road for a few hundred feet and fork left. Halfway around a circular road, on the left side, there is a gated trail into the forest.

Sources of additional information: The city hall of the town of Hollis, (603)

465-2209. If you're lucky, your call will be answered by the same nice woman I spoke with when I telephoned.

Notes on the trail: To do a counterclockwise loop, when you enter the forest off Patch Road take a right fork, then another right fork up a hill, then a left fork heading east. Continue in the same direction for about 1.5 miles, then veer left; you will eventually come out on a trail just behind the parking lot. If you head in the wrong direction in this compact forest you will soon arrive at a road. You can either double back to the last fork or take the paved road in the direction you're heading and pick up the next trail into the woods. (Some local residents know this forest as the "Dunklee Pond Conservation Area," after a pond located here.)

RIDE 30 *PISGAH STATE PARK*

This 15-mile ride circumvents about a third of a huge, undeveloped park. Three-quarters of the ride uses jeep roads; the remainder follows rougher trails with some wetness, and a mile or two of two-wheel-drive dirt roads.

These 13,000 acres of woods are full of rock outcroppings, wetlands, hemlock and birch trees, beaver ponds, swimming ponds, and wildlife (you'll see them if you're quiet). Head west for more trails (but don't ride on paths marked as biking-restricted). An active volunteer group, Friends of Pisgah, helps rangers to maintain the trails and bridges, and has an information center. They also sponsor open houses, picnics, and clean-ups (P.O. Box 1179, Keene, New Hampshire, 03431).

General location: In the southwestern tip of New Hampshire, between the towns of Chesterfield and Winchester.

Elevation change: The area is relatively flat with a fair amount of moderate climbing and descending on double- and single-track trails.

Season: Any time between early June and fall is good for riding. Pisgah is closed to off-road biking during the winter. State parks in New Hampshire officially open on May 23. There is plenty of mud in the spring.

Services: All services are available along NH 9 to the north, and in Keene, 8 miles to the east. There is no camping in the park.

Hazards: Be prepared to change riding techniques when switching from smoother paths to more rugged trails with loose rock and obstructions. In autumn, obstructions can be hidden by leaves. Mosquitoes can appear in late spring and summer. Check with a ranger to find out when hunting season begins in late fall.

Rescue index: You are never more than 3 miles from assistance.

Land status: State park roads and trails.

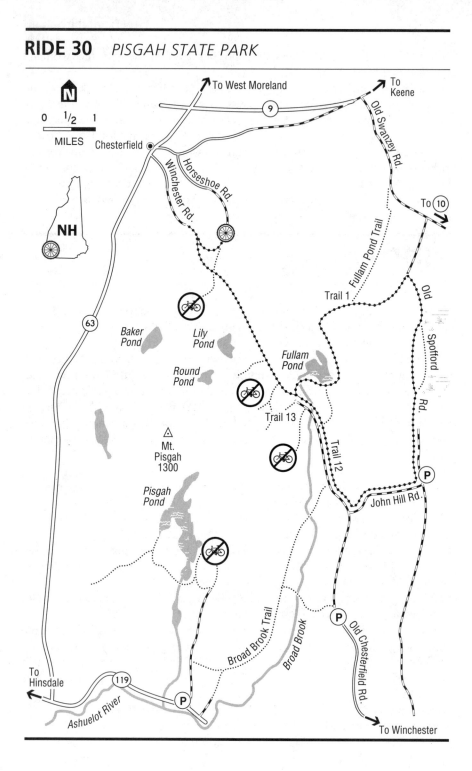

Maps: USGS, Winchester, New Hampshire. Trail maps are available at trailheads.

Finding the trail: From NH 9, turn south on NH 63. In Chesterfield, between the town hall and school, turn left onto Old Chesterfield Road and follow brown signs for Pisgah State Park. After two-tenths of a mile turn right onto Horseshoe Road. After another 1.6 miles you'll reach a parking lot with information and maps. There are four other parking areas around the park.

Sources of additional information:

Pisgah State Park
P.O. Box 242
Winchester, New Hampshire 03470
(603) 239-8153

Summers Backcountry Sports
16 Ashuelot Street
Keene, New Hampshire
(603) 357-5107

Notes on the trail: With a trail map you can follow many different loops in this large "park." But not all the trails in this park are open for biking. Obey signs restricting bikes. However, signs banning motorized dirt bikes and all-terrain vehicles (ATVs) do not apply to mountain bikes.

Here is one large loop ride. Take the double-track trail heading downhill out of the parking area (watching out for walkers). After a short distance veer left. You will pass a beaver pond on the right. If the trail is flooded, take a detour on a single-track trail on the left. At 2.5 miles, you pass a turn to the left toward Fullam Pond. This is where you'll come out at ride's end. (For a short out-and-back ride, turn left toward Fullam Pond.)

Veer right onto a two-wheel-drive dirt road (Old Chesterfield Road), which is maintained for vehicles bringing boats to Fullam Pond. (After about a mile you will pass a trail junction on the right marked "4." You can take this trail to the swimmable Pisgah Pond.) After another half mile or so you will reach a gate. Turn left onto an old asphalt road before you reach the gate. (If you go straight you will arrive at a parking lot and trailhead near the southern boundary of the park.) After about a mile you see a gate. Before reaching the gate, turn left onto a grassy trail. You will come out at another parking area on the east side of the park. Turn right out of the parking area and immediately left onto Old Spofford Road.

After about a mile, take a right fork downhill. The road may be flooded. If it is, take a single-track detour on the right, rejoin the road and go for about another half mile until you reach a break in a stone wall on the left. Turn left onto a trail that climbs, paralleling the road to avoid another flooded section. Rejoin the road, and when it veers right, turn left through a gate and onto an overgrown road going uphill. (You can ride back to the trailhead on easier roads by staying on the road, turning left on Old Swanzey Road, left again before NH 9, and left onto Horseshoe Road.)

Veer left at the junction with Trail 1. At the next fork you can turn right to reach Fullam Pond, or left to join Trail 12, then right on Trail 13, returning to the trailhead. Turning right toward the pond, you will cross a small dam and spillway. (There should be a log bridge across the spillway; if not, carry your bike across rocks just downstream from the spillway.) Ride around the southern shore of the pond and pick up a trail heading west that comes out on Trail 13— this is the junction you passed going the other way. Turn right and head uphill for about 2.5 miles to the parking area.

RIDE 31 *OLD MOUNTAIN ROAD*

This five-and-a-half-mile (out-and-back) ride is popular among local riders. The southern half of it uses a hard-packed dirt road, while the northern half tackles a heavily eroded former road that is now a fun trail. In the middle of the woods, side trails fork eastward toward Temple Mountain and NH 123 to the west. These side trails aren't well marked, so be ready to do some exploring if you try them.

At its northern terminus the ride comes out next to a farm, fields, and a pond. The southern trailhead is immediately across from the Sharon Arts Center, an arts and crafts gallery, crafts store, and performance center, where live music concerts happen in the summer, (603) 924-7256. A mile from the ride, on NH 101, Temple Mountain ski area holds mountain bike races and sometimes opens its trails for casual biking. Across from Temple Mountain more trails exist in Miller State Park and around Pack Monadnock Mountain.

General location: The town of Sharon on NH 123.
Elevation change: This out-and-back ride gains a total of about 400' in a single direction.
Season: Any time from mid-June to fall is good for riding. There is mud in the spring.
Services: Water, restrooms, and ice cream are available at Temple Mountain. All other services are available in Peterborough, 2 miles to the northwest.
Hazards: Be prepared to switch riding techniques in the middle of this ride, and watch for obstructions and deep ruts on the rugged half.
Rescue index: You are about a mile from assistance at the farthest.
Land status: Old town road.
Maps: A detailed state road map will do.
Finding the trail: The southern trailhead is across from the Sharon Arts Center

RIDE 31 *OLD MOUNTAIN ROAD*

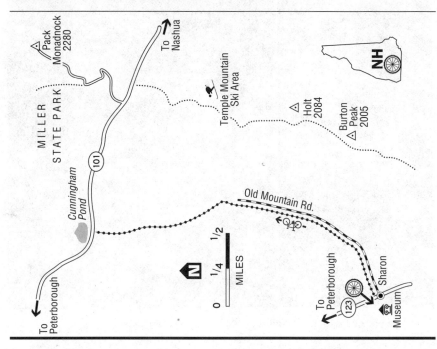

on NH 123, 3.6 miles south of the junction of NH 123 and NH 101. You can park in the parking lot next to the trailhead across from the center. (Do not use the parking lot on the same side of the road as the arts center.)

Sources of additional information:

Spokes and Slopes
30 Grove St.
Peterborough, New Hampshire 03458
(603) 924-9961

Temple Mountain Ski Area
Route 101
Peterborough, New Hampshire 03458
(603) 924-6949

Notes on the trail: Ride up Mountain Road across from the Sharon Arts Center. After 1.5 miles the road ends at a clearing and becomes a trail. (Novice riders can relax and turn around.) The trail begins with a steep uphill for about a half mile, flattens out, and then descends for about a half mile. When it comes out

A beckoning road sign at the trailhead. Sharon, New Hampshire.

at a grassy clearing, stay to the right and ride between two wooden fences. You pass by a house on the left and then a beaver pond on the right. Turn back, or climb the short, steep paved section to NH 101.

RIDE 32 *OLD KING'S HIGHWAY*

This eight-mile loop, with six more miles of side trails, alternates between abandoned byways through light woods and two-wheel-drive dirt roads through settled countryside. This is a moderately challenging ride: about two-thirds of it uses maintained dirt roads, but there's a fair amount of riding on overgrown roads and a challenging climb on a side trail.

A century ago, the abandoned roads at the beginning and end of this ride were main arteries between neighboring towns—hence "Old King's Highway." Today, you might catch a beaver surveying its pond along one of these secluded, overgrown roads. The most dramatic scenery comes on a side trail off Old Dublin Road, the Beeline Trail, which climbs to the top of a mountain. On the main loop you roll over dirt roads near the attractive town of Hancock. There is a

RIDE 32 *OLD KING'S HIGHWAY*

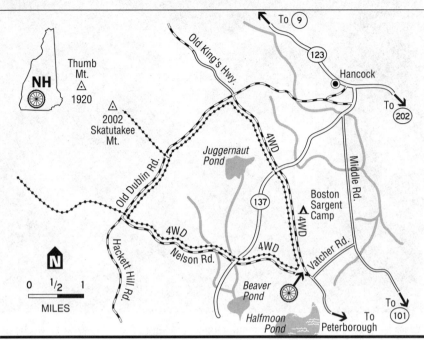

public swimming area at Halfmoon Pond. Before crossing the bridge on Windy Road turn left toward Sargent's Camp. The pond comes up on the right.

General location: Town of Hancock.

Elevation change: This is rolling terrain, with some moderate climbs. There is steeper climbing on side trails.

Season: This is a 4-season ride. Look out for mud in the spring.

Services: All services are available in Hancock and Peterborough to the south. Peterborough is a cultural and artistic center in southern New Hampshire. Spokes and Slopes, 30 Grove Street in Peterborough, (603) 924-9961, sponsors weekly mountain bike rides.

Hazards: Watch for hidden obstructions—ruts and logs—on the more rugged roads at the beginning and end of the ride. These abandoned byways are overgrown in late summer and fall. The first side trail is rocky and eroded, requiring technical climbing and descending skill.

Rescue index: You are never more than a mile from assistance.

Land Status: Town roads and old town roads.

Maps: USGS, Peterborough, NH (15 minute series).

Finding the trail: From Peterborough, take Union Street uphill and out of town. Turn right onto Windy Road. You will pass a sign on the left for Sargent's Camp

"Class VI" roads are unmaintained and unimproved—go for it. Hancock, New Hampshire.

and then cross a bridge. Park along the road after the bridge. A short distance farther, just as the road veers to the right, there is a left fork onto an overgrown road with a sign reading: "Road closed subject to gates and bars."

Sources of additional information:

> Spokes and Slopes
> 30 Grove St.
> Peterborough, New Hampshire 03458
> (603) 924-9961
>
> Temple Mountain Ski Area
> Route 101
> Peterborough, New Hampshire 03458
> (603) 924-6949
> This ski resort holds at least one mountain bike race each year.

Notes on the trail: Take the left fork onto the overgrown jeep trail at the trailhead and almost immediately another left fork onto the Washburn Trail. (You will see a faded sign for this trail.) The right fork is where this ride comes out. Go straight at another left fork and reach a paved road. Cross this fork onto another dirt road, Nelson Road. After another mile you reach a beaver pond and soon intersect a maintained dirt road with a house on the right. The main loop for this ride turns right. You can pedal straight ahead onto a steep, eroded trail, however, which reaches its summit after about 2 miles. Then turn around, descend, and turn left on Old Dublin Road.

After about another mile you will reach another side trail on the left, the Beeline Trail. This one is less challenging. You can stash your bike and hike up the last part for an excellent view—and blueberries in mid-summer. Then descend on the main loop for about a mile until you reach a narrow dirt road on the right with a sign reading: "Mud/Pass at own risk." Turn right on this road, Old King's Highway; you will almost immediately pass a small cinderblock building on the left with a sign: "Hancock Water Works." At a "T" junction go straight and slightly to the right, staying on the old dirt road. After another 1.5 miles or so you will reach the trailhead just before Windy Road.

RIDE 33   *HOPKINTON-EVERETT ALL-TERRAIN-VEHICLE TRAIL BIKE SYSTEM*

This lowland terrain has four large interconnecting loops designated for all-terrain vehicles (ATVs), which include both motorized dirt bikes and mountain bikes. You can ride anywhere from about 3 to 20 miles on these trails, which are marked from easy to difficult. Because of loose gravel and short, steep climbs, some "easy" trails can be moderate for mountain bikes and "moderate" trails can seem difficult. Although these trails are also open for motorized two- and three-wheeled vehicles, they're often unused.

This area lies in the middle of a marshland, with several waterways through it, plus ponds, a lake, meadows, pine woods, and wildlife. (Your greatest chance to see wildlife is in the morning and evening.) There is also swimming and picnicking at Clough State Park, abutting on the south.

General location: Town of Dunbarton, 6 miles southwest of Concord on NH 13.
Elevation change: Generally flat, but some trails have many short, steep hills.
Season: Any time between mid-summer and early winter is fine. Expect some muddy areas into June. Riding on these trails is not allowed from the end of snowmobile season (bare ground) to May 23.
Services: All services are available in Dunbarton and at the Dunbarton Country Store on the access road.
Hazards: Motorized off-road vehicles also use these trails. Yield to them, since you can hear them but they can't hear you. (They're a friendly lot, and the trails aren't crowded at all.) There is some loose sand and gravel on some trails. And on the marshland trails mosquitoes can be a nuisance in late spring and early summer.

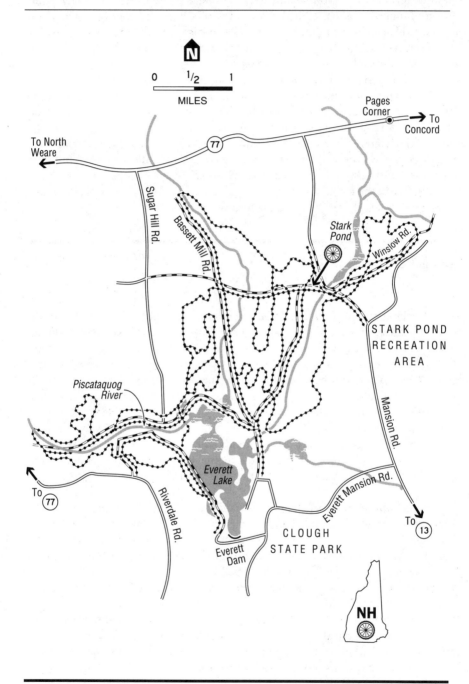

Rescue index: You are about 2 miles from roads at the farthest.

Land status: State-maintained trails.

Maps: A map of 6 ATV trails in New Hampshire is available from the Bureau of Off-Highway Vehicles: P.O. Box 856, 105 Loudon Road, Concord, New Hampshire, (603) 271-3254. A trail map is also posted at the parking lot. Topographical maps of New Hampshire are stocked at Gibson's Bookstore at 29 S. Main Street in Concord, (603) 224-0562.

Finding the trail: Take Exit 2 off Interstate 89, just outside Concord, and head south on NH 13. After 5 miles, about a mile past the intersection with NH 77, turn right immediately after the Dunbarton Country Store on the right. Coming from the south on NH 13, the turnoff is on the left about 3 miles north of Dunbarton. After seven-tenths of a mile take a right fork toward "OHRV Parking"; you will reach the parking lot after another seven-tenths of a mile.

Sources of additional information:

Park Office
Hopkinton-Everett Lake
Box 210, RR 2
Contoocook, NH 03229

Bureau of Trails
Division of Parks and Recreation
P.O. Box 1856
Concord, New Hampshire 03302
(603) 271-3254

Notes on the trail: Several trailheads fan off the parking area. To begin a longer, moderate loop, ride onto the dirt road next to the posted trail map. ("ATVs prohibited" signs on the roads do not apply to mountain bikes.) A trailhead comes up on the right after a few hundred feet. After that, trail junctions are marked. For an easy ride stay on the dirt roads through this reservoir area, heading west and south, toward Clough State Park and Everett Lake. Roads cross trails at several points.

NOTE: *Mountain Biking on All-Terrain Vehicle Trails in New Hampshire.* The state of New Hampshire has designated 6 trail systems for all-terrain vehicles— motorized dirt bikes, three-wheelers, and mountain bikes. Four of them are out-and-back rides, from 8 to 22 miles long, while the other 2 are loops. You can obtain a map of the 6 areas from the Bureau of Off-Highway Vehicles (P.O. Box 856, 105 Loudon Road, Concord, NH, (603) 271-3254). Maps may also be available at the trailheads. The Dunbarton Country Store on the access road may also carry this map.

The six state trail systems are:

1. Pisgah All-Terrain-Vehicle Trail Bike Area: off Route 119 near Pisgah State Park in Winchester. (See Pisgah State Park ride for directions.)
2. Rockingham Recreational Trail: 1.5 miles west on NH 28 from Windham near I-93.
3. Hopkinton-Everett Reservoir: off NH 13 south of the intersection with NH 77.
4. Sugar River Trail: at the Newport Recreation Department in Newport.
5. Success All-Terrain-Vehicle Trail Bike Area: 2 miles north on NH 16 from Berlin.
6. Cow Mountain ATV-Trail Bike Area: on NH 16 about 13 miles north of Berlin.

RIDE 34 *MASSABESIC LAKE / TOWER HILL POND*

You will enjoy mixing and matching parts of this ride: a 25-mile out-and-back "rail trail" (a former railroad bed), a 4.5-mile loop around a pond, and a more ambitious out-and-back ride north into a large state park. This ride links up with both the Newfields Rail Trail ride and the Bear Brook State Park ride.

The route begins on a maintained cinder path (the rail trail), then switches to dirt roads, and finally reaches smooth double-track trails around the pond. The trail (a major north-south snowmobile route) toward the state park is rougher. Along the ride you pass a large lake, pedal next to sunny clearings with wildflowers, birds, and ripe berries in summer, and enter woods around the pond. There is also a network of trails around Massabesic Lake.

General location: Two miles east of Manchester on NH 28.
Elevation change: This is a relatively flat ride with short, gradual climbs.
Season: Its ease and drainage make this a good 4-season ride.
Services: Water is available at the trailhead near the baseball field. There is also a convenience store in the traffic circle just before the trailhead. All other services are available in Manchester.
Hazards: None.
Rescue index: The route runs close to houses and roads, except for the optional trail north toward Bear Brook State Park, where you will be only a couple of miles from assistance.
Land status: A public rail trail (an abandoned railroad bed), service roads maintained by the Manchester Water Supply, and a snowmobile trail.
Maps: USGS, Candia, NH (1974).
Finding the trail: Take Exit 7 off Interstate 93, traveling on NH 101 east for only a short distance and get off on Exit 1. On NH 28 south go around a traffic circle and park along the road next to the playing field on the right, across from Massa-

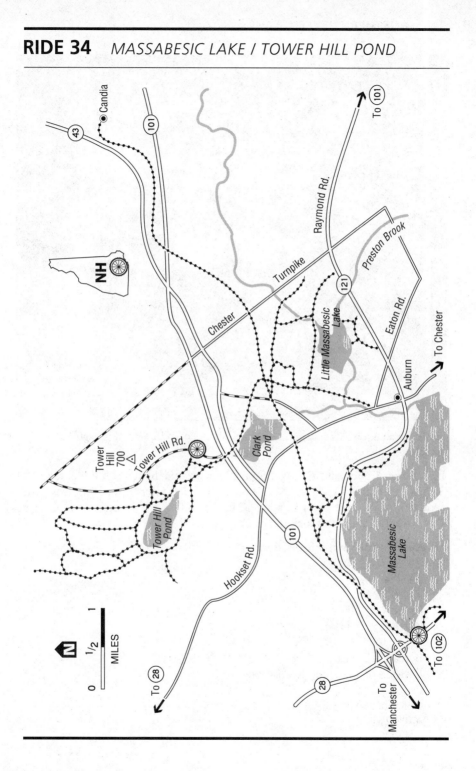

Playing in a puddle. Manchester, New Hampshire. *Photo by Fred McLaughlin.*

besic Lake. To do just the easy 4.5-mile loop around Tower Hill Pond, take NH 101 east to Exit 2. Turn right, then take the first left after about 200 yards. After four-tenths of a mile you will reach a small parking area on the left, near a gate at the trailhead. Don't block the gate.

Sources of additional information:

Nault's
30 Bridge St.
Mancester, NH
(603) 669-7993

Bureau of Trails
Division of Parks and Recreation
P.O. Box 1856
Concord, NH 03302
(603) 271-3254

Notes on the trail: The trailhead is on the left side of Massabesic Lake. After 3.2 miles riding on the rail trail there's a trail on the left with a brown sign: "Route 15 North." This is the trail to Tower Hill Pond and Bear Brook State Park. For an out-and-back ride, go straight on the rail trail. You will soon reach a short tunnel that is dark and wide-planked, but rideable, and then another longer, darker tunnel after another mile. This abandoned railroad bed runs east for another 20 miles (see the Newfields Rail Trail ride).

Heading north off the rail trail (3.2 miles from the trailhead), you will first cross a dirt road after a half mile, and then a paved road. Immediately after crossing the paved road and going under a bridge, take a small trail forking to the left up a short steep hill. Turn left and you will reach Tower Hill Pond at a dam. You can go in either direction around the pond.

After about 2 miles around the pond, a trail at a yellow gate just before a concrete bridge heads north toward Bear Brook State Park (see Bear Brook State Park ride). Continuing around the pond, you'll reach the other side of the dam. Turn right, cross the dam, and retrace your route to the rail trail.

NOTE: The Granite State Wheelmen. New Hampshire's largest bicycling club, the Granite State Wheelmen (GSW), now holds weekly off-road rides. Riding with the GSW is a good way to find out about other rides—and maybe hook up with a riding partner. Newcomers are welcome. The GSW puts out a newsletter listing weekly off-road rides. For more information drop in to a local bike shop and ask questions or pick up a newsletter.

RIDE 35 *NEWFIELDS RAIL TRAIL*

On this 25-mile rail trail you can ride for as long as you want, maintaining a leisurely or a fast pace. This former railroad bed is now a maintained gravel and dirt trail with a few dips, mounds, and minor obstructions. It is bordered by light woods, open fields with wildflowers, and private and commercial backyards. Because it's visible, patrolled, and well used, the trail is largely free of litter (litter can be a problem on some rail trails near populated areas). This accessible ride offers plenty of options. You can pick it up at many junctions and take a four-mile spur off to the south, into the town of Fremont.

General location: This trail runs through many towns across southern New Hampshire, from Newfields to just outside Manchester.
Elevation change: Flat.
Season: This is a 4-season ride.
Services: The trail crosses several commercial roads, with food and water at stores and gas stations.

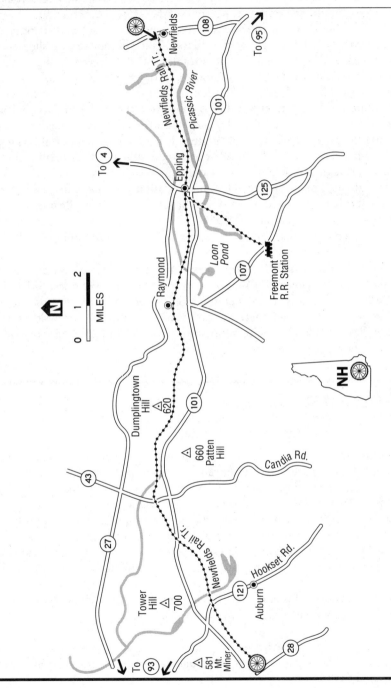

Darkness at the entrance of a tunnel. Newfields Rail Trail, Raymond, New Hampshire. *Photo by Fred McLaughlin.*

Hazards: Stop at all road crossings—motorists are not always expecting cyclists to come out of the woods.

Rescue index: You are always close to traveled roads.

Land status: This former Boston & Maine Railroad line is now a public right-of-way. A buried AT&T fiber optic line is also maintained here (as orange signs along the way indicate).

Maps: *The New Hampshire Atlas and Gazetteer* (DeLorme Mapping Co., Freeport, Maine, 04032), a collection of detailed maps of all the byways in the state, is available in many stores.

Finding the trail: You can begin riding at many intersecting streets. To start at the eastern terminus in Newfields, take NH 108 north from the junction with NH 85 for about a half mile. If you look to the left as you cross a high bridge, you can see an existing railroad line and an abandoned railroad station. Just after the bridge, turn left and go down a paved road, pass a golf course on the right, and come to the abandoned station. The trail begins behind the station, forking away from the railroad tracks.

To begin at the western terminus outside Manchester, see the Massabesic Lake/Tower Hill Pond ride, which begins at the same trailhead. You can also begin at the southern end of a 4-mile spur at the railroad station in Fremont on NH 107.

Sources of additional information:

Wheel Power
37 Water Street
Exeter, New Hampshire 03833
(603) 772-6343

Bureau of Trails
Division of Parks and Recreation
P.O. Box 1856
Concord, NH 03302
(603) 271-3254

The Rails-to-Trails Conservancy
1400 16th St., NW
Washington, D.C. 20036
(202) 797-5400
This is a national clearinghouse for rail trails.

Notes on the trail: At several intersections and parking lots the trail is broken for a short distance. You must find it on the other side of the intersecting pavement.

RIDE 36 *PAWTUCKAWAY STATE PARK*

This popular state park has a 12-mile loop with about 3 miles of side trails. The loop uses both double- and single-track trails and secluded dirt roads with a mile or two on a paved access road. It is a moderately challenging ride, with regular, short technical climbs and descents.

These 5,500 acres contain a lot of different landscapes. The Fundy Trail (on the eastern side of the park) runs along a marsh, where you might see beaver, deer, and great blue herons, especially in early morning and evening. A side trail to Fundy Cove reaches the shore of large Pawtuckaway Lake. On the other side of the park, a climb to the top of South Mountain is rewarded with panoramic views from a fire tower; on a clear day you can see the Atlantic Ocean. At the northern edge of the park another trail goes through a field of huge boulders, where local rock climbers hone their skills. There is also swimming at a 700-foot beach and 180 campsites.

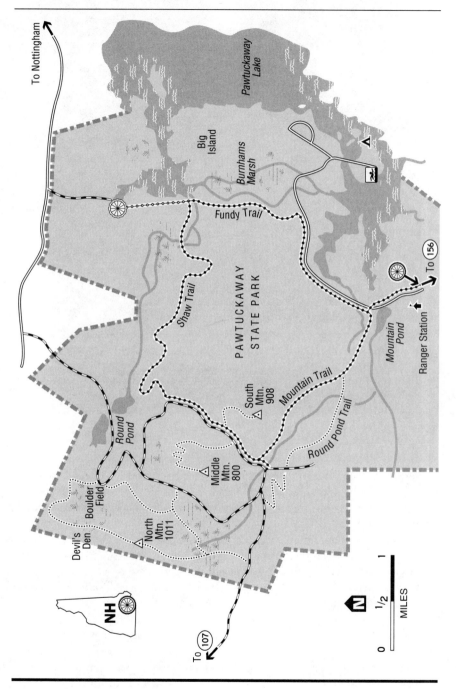

Descending on a single-track. Pawtuckaway State Park, Nottingham, New Hampshire.

General location: Nottingham, about 20 miles east of both Concord and Manchester.

Elevation change: The terrain is relatively flat, with short, gradual climbs on both trails and dirt roads.

Season: Local mountain bikers ride in this park year-round. During the winter a group ride leaves from the parking lot on Sunday mornings at 9A.M. Spring is muddy and summer can bring some mosquitoes.

Services: There is water at the park's information center. All other services are available in Nottingham to the north and Raymond to the south. There's also the Wheel Power bike shop on Water Street in Exeter, (603) 772-6343.

Hazards: Watch for hikers on the more popular trails near the parking area and be aware of obstructions on the single-track trails.

Rescue index: You are about a mile from a park road at the farthest.

Land status: State park roads and trails. *Note:* All trails in the park are open in the off-season—before Memorial Day and after Labor Day. During the summer and fall the park manager asks that mountain bikers stay off the popular Mountain Trail on weekends.

Maps: Trail maps are available at the park information center at the parking lot.

Finding the trail: From the south, take Exit 5 off NH 101, onto NH 156 north. Watch for brown state park signs. Turn left off NH 156 onto Mountain Road, which reaches the park entrance on the left after about a mile. You can also enter the park from the north and west (thus avoiding the $2.00 entrance fee, which is collected only in season). Enter off Route 107 on the west at a paved access road with a faded sign: "Pawtuckaway Lookout Tower."

Sources of additional information:

Park Manager
Pawtuckaway State Park
(603) 895-3031

New Hampshire Division of Parks and Recreation
P.O. Box 1856
Concord, New Hampshire 03302
(603) 271-3556

Notes on the trail: From the parking lot, head down a paved road and turn right, passing a toll booth (where you pay $2.00 from Memorial Day to Labor Day). After a 1.5-mile descent on pavement, take a left turn onto a dirt road when the pavement forks right. Keep to the left on a four-wheel-drive trail. After about 1.5 miles, just beyond a wooden bridge and marshy area, the main loop turns left at the "T" junction. Here you can take the first of several side trails. Heading right, you will arrive at a boat launching area on Pawtuckaway Lake. On the other side of the launching site, a dirt road heads along the lake to more serene areas along the lake. Then double back to the "T" junction where you could have turned left.

After a couple of miles on the Shaw Trail, you will come out on a road. Again the main loop turns left. If you head right, a side trail heads north for three-quarters of a mile to Devil's Den, through a field of giant boulders called "erratics," deposited when the glaciers melted at the close of the Ice Age about 15,000 years ago. A few hundred yards further on the main dirt road, there is another side trail on the left, which climbs to an excellent view. Watch out for hikers on this popular trail.

Just beyond that lefthand trail, where the road veers right, go straight onto another trail—Mountain Trail. This trail forks left, and after a mile or two, comes out on a paved road with a pond on the right. Turn right and head up the hill, past the toll booth, turning right into the parking lot.

RIDE 37 *HILLSBORO-HENNIKER*

This moderate 12-mile ride loops through both inhabited and uninhabited rural landscapes. It begins in a small town on a scenic paved road, bordered by long stone walls and broad fields. Then it switches to a rugged abandoned byway running through woods, linking up with another woods trail. After that, the ride stays mainly on two-wheel-drive roads while rolling past summer homes and large fields with good views of nearby mountains, before ending on a rolling trail next to a lively river. Finally, you ride past an outdoor antique truck museum and a popular ice cream and pizza shop. What more could you ask for?

General location: This trail runs through the adjoining towns of Hillsboro and Henniker.

Elevation change: The first third of the ride has regular short climbs and descents on pavement, trails, and dirt roads; then it is downhill and flat for the rest of the ride.

Season: Any time between mid-June and fall is good for riding. Expect some mud in spring.

Services: All services are available in Hillsboro and Henniker. A good place to stop is the Ped'ling Fool bike shop, 77 W. Main Street, Hillsboro, (603) 464-5286.

Hazards: There is a short, technical descent on a jeep trail at the beginning of the ride, and a short, steep descent on a dirt road that meets a busier paved road. Be prepared to switch riding techniques when changing from secluded trails to active roads.

Rescue index: Homes are nearby along this ride.

Land status: Town roads and old town roads.

Maps: The Ped'ling Fool bike shop in Hillsboro sells topographical maps and has them displayed on a wall.

Finding the trail: You can park at the Ped'ling Fool bike shop on W. Main Street (NH 9) in Hillsboro.

Sources of additional information: The Ped'ling Fool bike shop (77 W. Main St., Hillsboro, NH. 03244, (603) 464-5286) organizes rides, usually on weekends, from "easy rider" excursions to demanding 30-mile treks through the woods. Riders come from Boston to tackle the hills around Hillsboro.

Notes on the trail: Turn left off Main Street onto Church Street (one block from the Ped'ling Fool). At the end of the street ride carefully around the left side of the elementary school, and turn right on the paved road. At the intersection turn left onto School Street, heading north. After about a mile you wil pass a long stone wall on the left. Turn right onto an abandoned grassy road (Whitney Road), which comes out after about a half mile onto a new dirt road. Turn

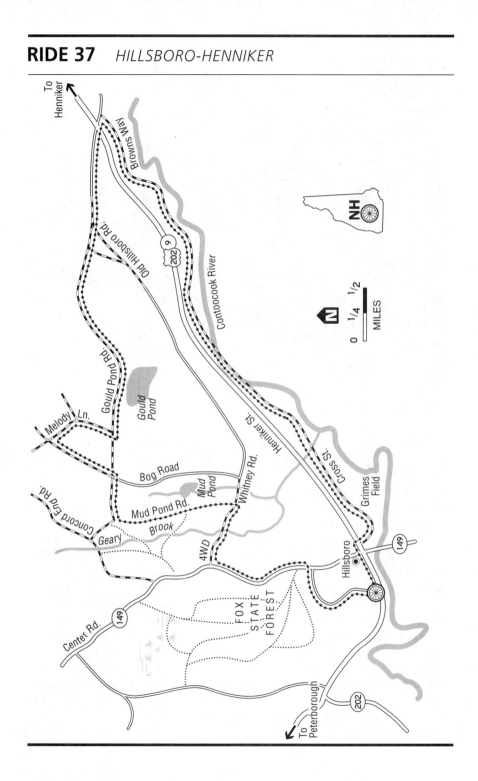

Getting the lowdown before a group ride. Hillsboro, New Hampshire.

left for only a few yards, then left onto a trail into the woods opposite a house. (There may be a sign at the trail reading: "To Mud Pond.") This trail becomes more challenging before coming out on Gould Pond Road. Turn right and come to an intersection. Turn left downhill on Bog Road. After crossing a bridge, turn right onto Cross Road. At the end, turn right onto Melody Lane (although a sign on the far left side of the road says "Patten Hill Road"). This dirt road reaches a "T" junction at Gould Pond Road again. Turn left, and fork left at a grassy island; go down a steep, washboarded hill, and come out at a paved road. (You can bypass this steep hill by taking a right at the island and then a left.) Turn left on the pavement.

After crossing NH 9, a major highway, turn right onto Browns Way and ride along the Contoocook River for several miles, until you come out on a paved road. Turn right on the pavement and almost immediately left onto the trail again. When the trail comes out behind a building on NH 9, ride along the highway on the left side for a few hundred feet, and turn left onto Preston Street. Go past a playing field on the left, and turn left onto River Street. You will pass several dozen old trucks at a truck museum. Turn right onto Bridge Street, ride uphill to W. Main Street, and turn left to return to the parking lot.

RIDE 38 *MINK HILLS*

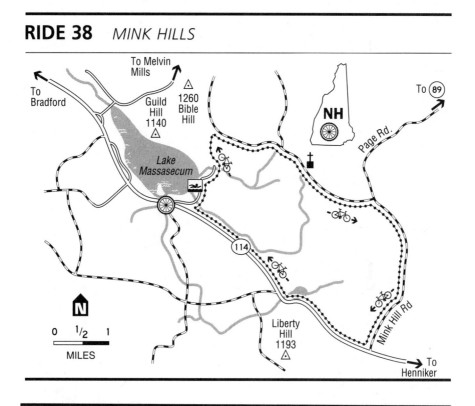

RIDE 38 *MINK HILLS*

This moderately challenging ten-mile loop includes a cruise along a lake, a technical one-mile climb on a double-track trail, more climbing on a secluded road, a steep descent on a rock-strewn four-wheel-drive road, and a 3.5-mile cruise back on a scenic, wide-shouldered highway.

You begin by riding past a public beach, summer homes, and a popular recreational lake. After passing more summer homes you will climb into the woods, cross a brook, and come out on a highland dirt road through what was once farmland. But today you will pass large maple, oak, hemlock, beech, and birch trees, an overgrown cellar hole or two, an occasional homestead, and an old cemetery surrounded by a stone wall. The cemetery is a good place to take a break, while admiring its stone steps and gravestones from the early 1800s. After negotiating a short wetland area and a rocky descent, you arrive back on the scenic highway bordered by wildflowers. Afterward, for a modest fee, you can use the public beach or rent a boat at the lake.

General location: Six miles north of Henniker, on NH 114.

Elevation change: This ride gains about 500' on both a trail and dirt road, before a steep descent on an eroded road.

Season: Any time between mid-June and fall is good for riding.

Services: The Lake Massasecum casino provides food and camping. All other services are available in Henniker, 6 miles to the south, and Bradford, 3 miles to the north.

Hazards: Watch out for plenty of loose rocks on the final descent on a jeep road. And mosquitoes can be present in late spring and summer.

Rescue index: You are never more than a mile from assistance.

Land status: Active and abandoned town roads.

Maps: USGS, Hillsboro, NH (15 minute series). *The New Hampshire Atlas and Gazetteer* (DeLorme Mapping Co., Freeport, ME, 04032), a collection of detailed maps of all byways in the state, is available in many stores.

Finding the trail: Park along NH 114, at the boat launching site at Lake Massasecum, 5.3 miles north of the junction of NH 114 and NH 9 and across from the access road to the Lake Massasecum campground.

Sources of additional information: The Pedaling Fool bike shop on 77 W. Main Street in Hillsboro is a popular meeting place for mountain bikers. It has maps, information about other rides in the area, and regular group rides. Phone: (603) 464-5286.

Notes on the trail: Take the paved access road that veers to the right of Lake Massasecum past summer homes. Veer right past a public beach and camping area and immediately turn left. After another half mile, fork right on a sandy road and climb. At the end of the road, continue straight into the woods on a trail, climbing for about eight-tenths of a mile. Coming out at a "T" junction on a dirt road turn right, veer right at a fork after about a mile, and pass an old cemetery on the left. About a mile past the cemetery, fork to the left, and almost immediately take a sharp right. This is the beginning of a 2.5-mile descent. After about a mile, you encounter a short stretch of fairly deep water. It's rideable, but for the sake of your bike you might want to carry it across. You will come out on NH 114. Turn right and return to Lake Massasecum on this well-paved highway with a wide, smooth shoulder.

RIDE 39 *NEWBURY LINE*

This easy out-and-back ride is a quick getaway in the woods along a former railroad line. The 6.5-mile round-trip uses a gravel, cinder, and sandy double-track trail through a forest of birches, beeches, and maples—a riot of color in autumn. Near the Newbury end you ride through a small granite pass that was blasted out with nitroglycerine in 1870, a major undertaking at that time. Look

RIDE 39 *NEWBURY LINE*

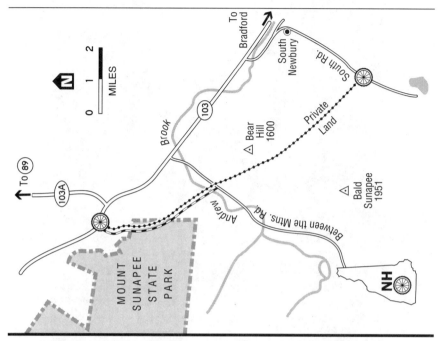

for mica sparkling in its granite walls and horsehair lichen hanging off it. Lake Sunapee, at the Newport end, has a public beach and ski mountain.

In the 1800s, many towns in New Hampshire ran their own railroads. The Civil War turned New Hampshire into a state that produced all kinds of goods that Americans wanted, and the railroads were the way to transport them. Just south of Newbury the railroad hit a wall, literally. Extending the line meant drilling and blasting through a solid granite wall. Today, the job would be almost trivial. But 120 years ago it took twelve months to bust through. The line was a commercial success. In 1961 the last engine pulled a load of tourists in an attempt to revive interest in train travel. But the highways had won out.

General location: Newbury.
Elevation change: Flat. Actually, it's a very gradual ascent to the north.
Season: Any time between May and the fall is good for riding.
Services: All services are available in Newbury or Bradford, 3 miles to the south on NH 103.
Hazards: None, except for some loose sand that requires concentration.
Rescue index: Although the trail passes through secluded woods, it is easy to get on and off, and runs within a mile of traveled roads.

Riding through a solid granite cut. Newbury, New Hampshire.

Land status: An abandoned railroad bed.

Maps: A detailed state road map will show the access roads.

Finding the trail: You can begin this ride at either terminus. From the north, pick it up just north of the junction of NH 103 and NH 103A, at the southern tip of Lake Sunapee, behind a restaurant and trading post on the left side of the road and across from a public dock and parking area. From the south, turn left off NH 103 at a white sign for South Newbury Village, 3.3 miles north of its junction with NH 114. Turn right immediately onto Village Road, and then left onto South Road. After 1 mile you will reach the trailhead, which is marked by several large boulders across the trail on the left. (Heading south from South Road, the rail trail becomes sandier and ends at a new dirt road after 1.5 miles.)

Sources of additional information:

Bob Skinner's Ski and Sport

Route 103
Mt. Sunapee, NH 03772
(603) 763-2303

RIDE 40 *BEAR BROOK STATE PARK*

This large, 9,500-acre park has about 40 miles of rideable trails. The trails become more rugged as they run deeper into the woods to the southwest, and narrower side trails are more challenging. Located just eight miles from Concord (the state capital), this popular state park has many marshes, ponds, brooks, and different woodscapes, depending on whether you're in the lowlands or highlands. There's also swimming, hiking, camping, fishing, and ski touring in the park.

The ride can be linked with the Massabesic Lake/Tower Hill Pond ride, by using a major north-south snowmobile trail, Route 15. (Snowmobile routes are often named after nearby roadways.) When this trail leaves the park to the south it crosses private land, so be sure to stay on the trail.

General location: Allenstown, on NH 28.
Elevation change: The trails in this state park are fairly level, with occasional short climbs.
Season: You can ride here in all seasons, although trails can be muddy in spring.
Services: The park has restrooms, water, and 80 tent sites. All other services are available along NH 28 and in Concord.
Hazards: Watch out for hikers, especially near the trailheads, and riding should be avoided during the late fall hunting season.
Rescue index: You will be about 5 miles from assistance at the farthest.
Land status: Public state park trails.
Maps: Pick up a trail map at park headquarters, or contact the New Hampshire Division of Parks and Recreation, 105 Loudon Rd., Concord, NH, 03301, (603) 271-3556.
Finding the trail: The entrance to the park is on NH 28, 3 miles north of its junction with US 3. Park in an unpaved lot located one-third of a mile up the access road on the right. One trail enters the woods on the left side of the parking area.

Sources of additional information:

New Hampshire Division of Parks and Recreation
P.O. Box 1856
Concord, NH 03302
(603) 271-3556

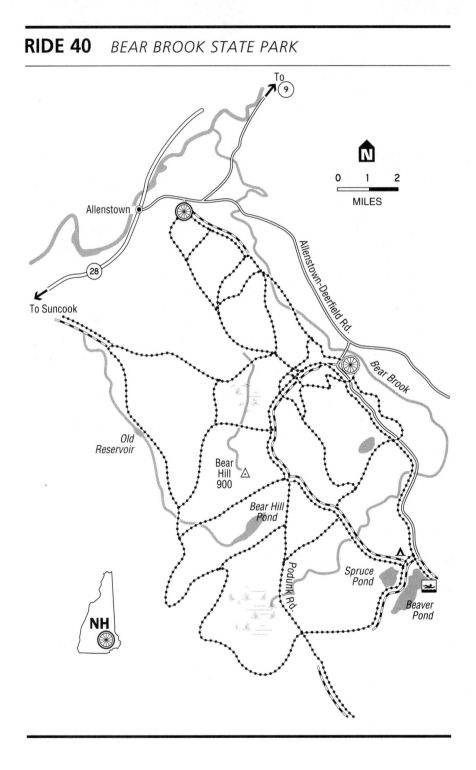

Bear Brook State Park
R.R.1, Box 507
Allenstown, NH 03275
(603) 485-9874

Notes on the trail: The access road is on the northern border of the park, so ride southward. This map shows a 20-mile loop that begins at the access road parking lot. Many trails are marked and numbered. You might want to stay on the wider, numbered trails. If you become disoriented, ride west to reach another trail or NH 28. There is also a major north-south snowmobile trail, Route 15, passing through the park, and linking up with the Massabesic Lake/Tower Hill Pond ride to the south.

RIDE 41 *BLUE JOB MOUNTAIN*

This 8.5-mile loop lies at the center of many more miles of dirt roads, especially to the west and south. (Check out other loops around Barn Door Gap, Parker Mountain, and Evans Mountain.) You can also do a side trip on this loop to Blue Job Mountain State Forest, which has a wildlife management area.

About half of the ride uses two-wheel-drive dirt roads, with some washboarding, and the other half tackles more rugged jeep roads. The ride switches from a rural setting of homes, fields, a handsome pond, and a reservoir, to a more secluded wooded landscape.

General location: Farmington, 6 miles west of Rochester.
Elevation change: This is rolling terrain, with some short climbs and descents.
Season: Any time between mid-June and fall is good for riding.
Services: All services are available in Rochester, 6 miles to the west.
Hazards: Watch out for light traffic on the two-wheel-drive roads and occasional minor obstructions on the jeep roads.
Rescue index: You are never more than a mile from assistance.
Land status: Active town roads and old town roads.
Maps: A collection of detailed, non-topographical maps of all byways in the state, *The New Hampshire Atlas and Gazetteer* (DeLorme Mapping Co., Freeport, ME, 04032), is available at many stores.
Finding the trail: Take Exit 13 off US 4, onto US 202 west. After 1.2 miles, turn right onto Estes Road. After about 4 miles the road becomes unpaved at an intersection where several mailboxes stand. Continue straight for a short distance until you reach a wider, more secluded section of the road, and park in that area.

RIDE 41 *BLUE JOB MOUNTAIN*

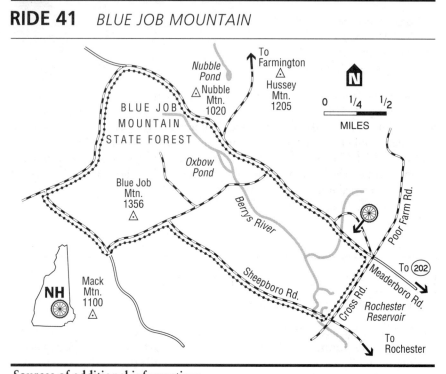

Sources of additional information:
Wheel Power
37 Water Street
Exeter, New Hampshire 03833
(603) 772-6343

Notes on the trail: At the intersection you passed before parking, head south-west on Cross Road. Soon after passing a reservoir on the right, turn right up a four-wheel-drive road. After about 2 miles turn left and continue for another half mile, until you reach a "T" junction, with a paved road on the left and a hard-packed dirt road on the right. Turn right and at the next intersection turn right again. The road then becomes more rugged. After another mile you will arrive at an intersection with pavement on the left and an unpaved road on the right. Turn right, pass a pond on the right, and after 1.8 miles you'll pass a right turn. Keep going straight to complete the loop. Or turn right onto a more rugged road, and reach an access road on the right running into Blue Job Mountain State Forest.

RIDE 42 BOSTON LOT LAKE

Here is a 5.5-mile loop that ends up at a "hidden" lake, just a few miles from busy Hanover and Lebanon and Interstates 91 and 89. The ride begins on a trail through light woods, climbs on a more challenging path, and reaches a lake circumvented by a tight single-track trail. Then you can descend the same way you came up, or else loop back on a steep gravel road and a paved road.

General location: Lebanon, on NH 10, 4 miles north of the junction of Interstates 89 and 91.

Elevation change: It is a short, fairly steep climb to the lake and a short, steep descent on a gravel road. The ride gains a total of about 300'.

Season: Mid-June through fall is best. Avoid riding here in spring because of mud on these delicate trails.

Services: All services are available in West Lebanon and Hanover.

Hazards: Less experienced riders should be prepared to walk on some sections of the trail around the lake. Also, the steep, loose gravel road descending from the lake has 2 iron bars across it. Be prepared for them.

Rescue index: You are about a half mile from assistance at the farthest.

Land status: State road, town road, and a trail open to the public.

Maps: USGS, Hanover, NH.

Finding the trail: On NH 10, 4 miles north of its junction with I-89, turn right after a large playing field on the right, onto Gould Road toward Sachem Village. Park along this road next to the field on the right, or at a gravel turnoff on the left.

Sources of additional information:

Omer & Bob's Sportshop
7 Allen Street
Hanover, New Hampshire 03755
(603) 643-3525

Tom Mowatt Cycles
3 High Street
Lebanon, New Hampshire 03766
(603) 448-5556
and Olde Nugget Alley
Hanover, New Hampshire 03755
(603) 643-5522
Mountain bikers meet for weekly rides at Tom Mowatt's shops.

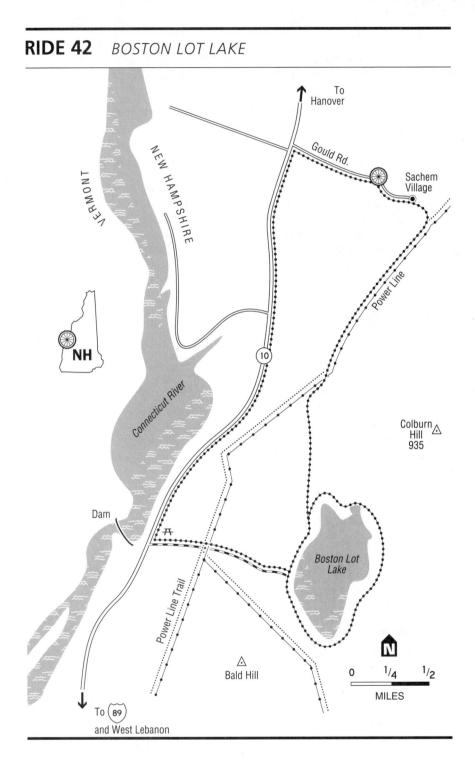

Climbing on a power line. Lebanon, New Hampshire.

Dartmouth College Outing Club
(603) 646-2428
The Outing Club of Dartmouth College has information about mountain biking in the Upper Valley, the area around the Connecticut River from about Hanover to Woodstock, Vermont. This Ivy League outdoor center is located in a Dartmouth College building on the green in Hanover.

Notes on the trail: At the end of Gould Road take a single-track trail across a grassy plot into the woods. Turn right immediately onto a wide power line trail. When the trail soon veers right, go straight onto a single-track trail. Then fork left onto a four-wheel-drive road that climbs steeply. Fork right and then right again. After cruising along a ridge turn right at an opening, and then left to reach the lake.

Follow blue and white blazes around the lake in either direction. The trail may seem to disappear on the other side of the lake, for a hundred feet or so, but it's there. When you return to the west side of the lake, head down the gravel road, which comes out at a parking area and picnic tables on NH 10, across from a dam. Turn right to return to Gould Road. Local drivers are used to cyclists on this paved road. But be attentive—don't push your luck. You never know when an out-of-state motorist might appear.

RIDE 43 *ORANGE COVE TRAIL / MT. CARDIGAN STATE PARK*

This 2.5-mile abandoned road, with an optional four-mile extension on its northern end, is a relatively easy out-and-back ride at the foot of a mountain. After about a half mile, this four-wheel-drive road turns into a rocky double-track trail, climbing gently through light woods and passing a large secluded pond. On the right, views of Mt. Cardigan break through the trees.

A couple of miles farther up the paved access road for this ride is a parking lot with several trailheads for the summit of Mt. Cardigan. Mountain biking on these popular hiking trails is difficult and not encouraged, but the bald summit has panoramic views. It's worth the hike.

General location: Town of Orange.
Elevation change: The ride climbs gradually for a hundred feet or so.
Season: Any time between mid-June through fall is good for riding.
Services: All services are available in Canaan and along US 4.
Hazards: Watch for occasional vehicles near the trailhead.
Rescue index: At the farthest you are about 2 miles from assistance.
Land status: An abandoned town road.
Maps: USGS, Cardigan, NH (15 minute series). *The New Hampshire Atlas and Gazetteer* (DeLorme Mapping Co., Freeport, ME, 04032), a collection of non-topographical maps of all byways in the state, is available at many stores.
Finding the trail: From US 4 take NH 118 north, forking right toward signs for Mt. Cardigan State Park. After about 2.5 miles you will cross a bridge, and turn left onto an old paved road. After another 1.2 miles the road becomes a four-wheel-drive road, which may have a cable across it. This cable is not meant to restrict cyclists. You can park on a small shoulder along the road after the last house on the left, or, if the cable is down, you can drive up the jeep road for a short distance to a clearing on the right.

Sources of additional information:

> Greasey Wheel
> 40 S. Main Street
> Plymouth, New Hampshire 03264
> (603) 536-3655
> This shop is a mecca for mountain bikers in central New Hampshire. It has lots of information, maps, and group rides.

RIDE 43 *ORANGE COVE TRAIL / MT. CARDIGAN STATE PARK*

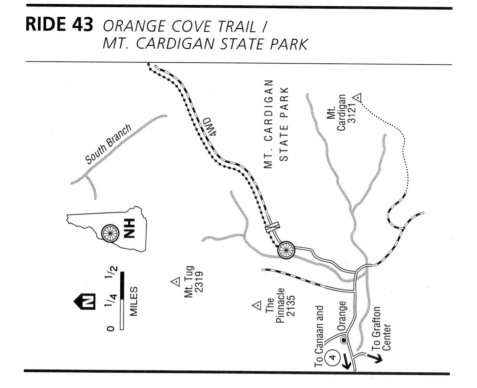

Notes on the trail: This narrow, rugged old road, called Orange Cove Trail, ends near a pond. Local riders claim that a trail at its end continues for another 4 miles to Sculptured Rocks Road to the northeast. It is downhill in that direction, requiring climbing skill to return.

RIDE 44 *PERCH POND / CASCADE-RIDGEPOLE TRAIL*

This eight-mile loop will challenge even the most experienced mountain biker with its steep single-track trails that turn and twist, running tightly through deep woods. Still, the loop is short enough that non-expert riders can do it, but they should plan to do some walking.

The first 2.5 miles of the ride follow a two-wheel-drive dirt road. Then you climb, ride on a ridge, and descend on single-track trails through a hardwood forest.

On the ridge you will reach two lookouts with good views of huge Squam Lake to the southeast. The views are on boulders a few feet from the trail on the

RIDE 44 *PERCH POND / CASCADE-RIDGEPOLE TRAIL*

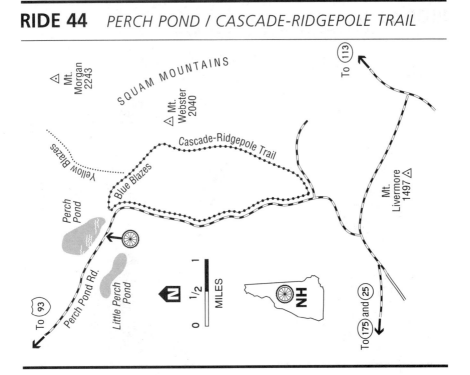

right (see "Notes on the trail"). Also, on the descent you pass a small waterfall at a junction in the woods.

General location: Seven miles northeast of Plymouth and 5 miles from Interstate 93.

Elevation change: This ride begins with a 2.5-mile warm-up on a rolling dirt road. Then it gains 1,050' on steep single-track trails. The last half of the ride descends, steeply at times.

Season: Any time between mid-June and fall is good for riding.

Services: All services are available in Plymouth, 7 miles to the south.

Hazards: Watch out for obstacles on the trails—encroaching trees, rocks, stumps, and holes—especially on the descent. Be prepared for mosquitoes in late spring and summer.

Rescue index: While riding the secluded trails in this somewhat remote area you are about 3 miles from assistance.

Land status: Active town road and public trails.

Maps: USGS, Squaw Mountains, NH. A map of rides in the area is available at the Greasey Wheel bike shop, 40 S. Main St., Plymouth, NH, 03264, (603) 536-3655.

Finding the trail: Take Exit 25 off I-93, and head north on NH 175. After 5 miles,

Fellow trail users in the White Mountain National Forest. Pinkham Notch, New Hampshire.

turn right after a large statue of a bear in front of a gift shop. Veer right, then left, staying on the main road (Perch Pond Road). After 3 miles you will reach the trailhead at a parking area on the left, at Perch Pond.

Sources of additional information:

Greasey Wheel
40 S. Main Street
Plymouth, New Hampshire 03264
(603) 536-3655
This shop is a mecca for mountain bikers in the southern White Mountains. It offers maps, information, and group rides.

White Mountain National Forest
Pemigewasset Ranger Station
RFD #3, Box 15, Route 175
Plymouth, New Hampshire 03264
(603) 536-1310

Notes on the trail: About three-quarters of the way into this ride there is one tricky turn. While descending in deep woods, fork left off the Crawford-

Ridgepole Trail (yellow blazes) onto the Cascade Trail (blue blazes). The junction is marked by a small waterfall on the right. Watch for it.

This ride begins on gravelly Perch Pond Road. At the bottom of a long downhill, turn left onto Mountain Road. When the road turns right after two-tenths of a mile, climb straight ahead on a trail. At the top of a steep climb, turn left onto Crawford-Ridgepole Trail, which is marked with a yellow sign on a tree on the left. After about a mile you will reach a lookout on the right, a few feet off the trail on the other side of several large boulders. It is a good view of Squam Lake. Another lookout comes up farther along the ridge.

After about another mile, at the end of a steep downhill, look for the left turn onto Cascade Trail. If you go by the Cascade Trail, riding becomes very difficult as you begin to climb another mountain. The single-track Cascade Trail eventually becomes a logging road with a stream on the left. Veer to the left, then right onto a grassy road, and you come out on Perch Pond Road just above Perch Pond.

RIDE 45 *GUINEA POND TRAIL / FLAT MOUNTAIN POND TRAIL*

This popular 17-mile (round-trip) out-and-back ride climbs gently and steadily on two long trails, becoming progressively more difficult. You can go as far as you want. These double-track trails, which are also popular with hikers, become rugged in places, with several stream crossings over makeshift bridges, some mud holes, a swampy area at the beginning, and some sections of loose rock.

Along the way, you will pass dramatic and varied woodscapes, including a secluded beaver pond, a gorge, and a highland pond. There is an Appalachian Mountain Club (AMC) shelter at Flat Mountain Pond. Overnight lodging there is on a first-come, first-served basis, and can be tight on weekends.

General location: Ten miles north of Plymouth, 6 miles east of Interstate 93.

Elevation change: It is a steady, not-too-steep climb for several miles.

Season: Any time between mid-June and fall is good for riding. Fall is the most colorful season. There's mud in spring and any season after heavy rains.

Services: Bring plenty of water—even clear streams can contain harmful bacteria. All services are available in Campton, 4 miles to the north, or Plymouth 10 miles to the south.

Hazards: Be prepared for some short, fast climbs before and after stream crossings. Also watch out for hikers. There can be leeches in the ponds, so don't swim in them.

Rescue index: This is a fairly well-traveled trail. At the farthest you're about 8 miles from help.

Land status: White Mountains National Forest trails.

RIDE 45 *GUINEA POND TRAIL / FLAT MOUNTAIN POND TRAIL*

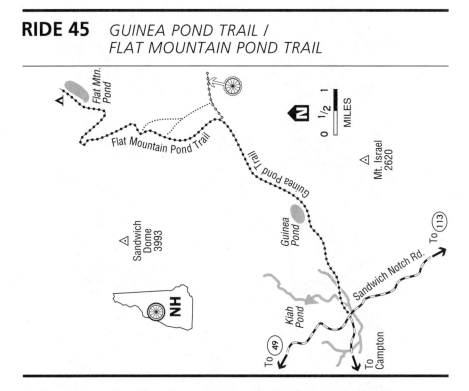

Maps: USGS, Waterville Valley, NH. The Appalachian Mountain Club (AMC) publishes a detailed trail book, *The AMC White Mountain Guide*. Also, a map of rides in the region is sold by the Greasey Wheel bike shop at 40 S. Main Street in Plymouth, (603) 536-3655.

Finding the trail: From Interstate 93 take Exit 28 to NH 49 east. After 4 miles take a steep right uphill onto Sandwich Notch Road. After 4 miles on this nearly four-wheel-drive road, just after a small bridge, you reach the trailhead, which is marked with several small trail signs. A few hundred feet beyond the trailhead on the right there is a sandy parking area. One caution: Sandwich Notch Road is not well maintained, so be prepared to maneuver around potholes and ruts. You can also reach the trailhead from the other direction on Sandwich Notch Road. To do so, take Diamond Ledge Road out of Sandwich for about a mile, and then fork left. From that direction the road is a bit smoother and a mile shorter.

Sources of additional information:

Greasey Wheel
40 S. Main Street
Plymouth, New Hampshire 03264
(603) 536-3655

Heading deeper into the forest. Flat Mountain Pond Trail, Sandwich, New Hampshire.

This shop is a mecca for mountain bikers in the southern White Mountains. It offers maps, information, and group rides.

White Mountain National Forest
Pemigewasset Ranger Station
RFD #3, Box 15, Route 175
Plymouth, New Hampshire 03264
(603) 536-1310

Saco Ranger Station
Route 112
Kancamagus Highway

Conway, New Hampshire
(603) 447-5448

Notes on the trail: These 2 trails are signed, making them fairly easy to follow. About a quarter mile from the trailhead, however, you will come to a beaver pond that sometimes floods the trail. If it has, take a single-track trail on the right around it. After about 2 miles you will begin following signs for the Flat Mountain Pond Trail.

NOTE: *Building Mountain Bike Trails in the White Mountains.* Two trails have been built in the White Mountain National Forest especially for mountain biking: the Brown Ash Swamp Trail and Dickey Notch Trail (still in progress). Together they're part of a trail system from Plymouth to the Kancamagus Highway. Designed for experienced riders, they were constructed from abandoned logging roads by local mountain biking enthusiasts working with the U.S. Forest Service. These "activists" have been organizing rides and cultivating friendships with other trail users and landowners in the White Mountains since the early 1980s. They also produce a map of mountain bike rides. To obtain a map visit the Greasey Wheel in Plymouth, (603) 536-3655. Two other good bike shops are Mountain Valley Bikes in Waterville Valley, (603) 236-4666, and Riverside Bikes in Ashland, (603) 968-9676. Or contact the Pemigewasset Ranger Station, RFD #3, Box 15, Route 175, Plymouth, NH, 03264, (603) 536-1310.

RIDE 46 *RESERVOIR POND / CUMMINS POND*

This 8- to 12-mile excursion combines an out-and-back ride on dirt roads and a loop in the middle on a rugged double-track trail. It begins at a popular parking area for hikers coming down from or heading up Smarts Mountain (3,238') on the famous Appalachian Trail. You will be climbing, steeply at first, on the dirt road, soon passing a pond with summer homes around it and good views of Smarts Mountain. Next you enter a private conservation area (bicyclists allowed). After looping through the woods you reach the summit of the ride at a waterfall tumbling out of Cummins Pond (1,526'). The return ride can be a screaming descent. Also, there is a public swimming spot at Reservoir Pond (look for an opening between two homes on the road).

General location: Three miles east of Lyme and ten miles north of Hanover.
Elevation change: This ride gains a total of about 700', mainly on two-wheel-drive dirt roads. The steepest part of this ride is at the beginning.
Season: Any time from mid-spring through fall is good for riding. There's shade in summer and you can swim if you wish. And there are lovely views in the fall.
Services: All services are available in Lyme and 10 miles south in Hanover.

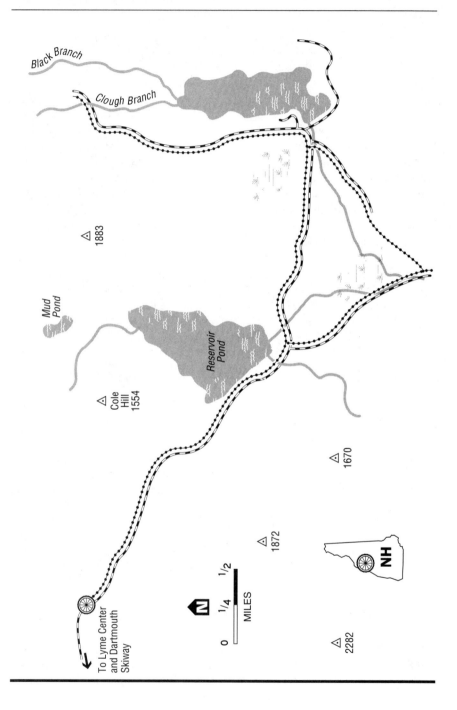

Black Branch

Clough Branch

△ 1883

Mud
Pond

△ Cole
Hill
1554

Reservoir
Pond

△ 1670

△ 1872

N

1/4   1/2

0   MILES

NH

△ 2282

To Lyme Center
and Dartmouth
Skiway

Take note of signs. This one reads: "Respect owner's property! Keep our land and waters clean. Do not damage or litter." Lyme, New Hampshire.

Hazards: Watch out for vehicles when descending on the two-wheel-drive road and for ruts on the overgrown trail in the middle of the ride.

Rescue index: Summer cabins are close by, except on the 2.5-mile loop, where you will be about a half mile from assistance.

Land status: A town road and a private road in the Laffer Woodlands. Mountain bikers have permission to use the roads through this private conservation land. Be considerate and leave nothing but tracks on the roads and trails.

Maps: USGS, Smarts Mountain, NH.

Finding the trail: Take NH 10 into Lyme (10 miles north of Hanover). Turn right toward Lyme Center, and after 3 miles you will reach a fork at Dorchester Road and the Dartmouth Skiway. If you go past a green building in a clearing at the Dartmouth Skiway, turn around and take the left fork onto Dorchester Road. After 1.7 miles you will reach a parking lot on the left, next to a stream. This is the trailhead for the Appalachian Trail going up Smarts Mountain. Park here and ride up the road.

Sources of additional information:

Omer & Bob's Sportshop
7 Allen Street

Hanover, New Hampshire 03755
(603) 643-3525

Tom Mowatt Cycles
Olde Nugget Alley
Hanover, New Hampshire 03755
(603) 643-5522

Notes on the trail: Riding up this two-wheel-drive road you will reach Reservoir Pond on the right after 1.5 miles. After another half mile you can continue straight or do a loop by turning right on another slightly more rugged two-wheel-drive road marked: "To Cummins Pond." After about a mile on this rougher road turn left just before a clearing, climb a short hill, and turn left again on a rutted, overgrown road, toward the sign: "Wentworth." You will come out at a logged clearing. Take the road on the other side of the clearing, ride over a stream, and turn right at a "T" junction. Head uphill and reach Cummins Pond and the main dirt road at a waterfall.

To extend the ride, turn left and pass through an opening into a field on a four-wheel-drive road. This is privately owned conservation land, so swimming (as well as camping and fires) are not allowed. You can travel northward on this secluded dirt road for several miles, until it becomes a hiking trail to Smarts Mountain. It becomes muddier. Then turn back and take a right, heading down the same way you came, but taking a right fork toward Reservoir Pond to complete the loop.

RIDE 47 *WILDERNESS TRAIL*

This easy 6.5-mile ride goes up and down both sides of a river on a popular trail and a dirt road. It is a convenient, scenic ride into the White Mountain National Forest. The flat, wide Wilderness Trail is also a popular hiking path. To do a loop ride, you must cross the river on a line of large boulders and carry your bike up a short, steep embankment.

On the west side of the Pemigewasset River, you ride on a trail that is actually an old railroad bed. You can either ride next to or "get some air" riding over the half-buried railroad ties. On the eastern shore of the river you will ride on a dirt access road. A well-marked side trail off the Wilderness Trail (west side) leads to Franconia Falls, a chute of water spilling over giant boulders on which you can walk and lie down. (You may want to stash your bike and walk up the last part of this popular side trail—see "Notes on the trail.")

General location: On the Kancamagus Highway (NH 112), 5 miles east of Interstate 93.

RIDE 47 *WILDERNESS TRAIL*

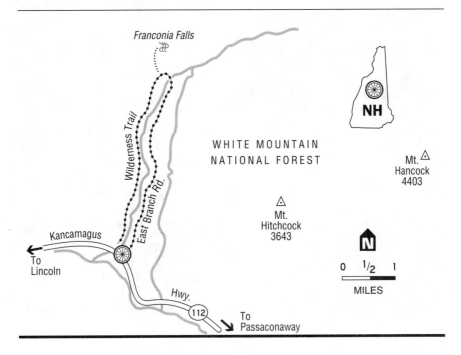

Elevation change: This ride climbs gently for 300′.

Season: Any time from late May through winter is good for riding.

Services: All services are available in Lincoln, 3 miles to the west on NH 112.

Hazards: If you do this ride as a loop, using both sides of the river, you must carry your bike up or down a short, steep embankment, and cross the river on a line of large boulders. It is not that difficult, but requires some balancing skill. Also, be careful not to startle walkers when passing them from behind. Rangers also recommend that you lock your car in this busy parking lot.

Rescue index: This well-traveled trail is patrolled by rangers.

Land status: Trail and access road in the White Mountain National Forest.

Maps: USGS, Mt. Osceola, NH. Also, the "Trail Map & Guide to the White Mountain National Forest" (DeLorme Publishing Co., Box 298, Freeport, ME, 04032) is a good trail map, available in many stores, including the Appalachian Mountain Club (AMC) lodge on the Kancamagus Highway: Pinkham Notch Camp, P.O. Box 298, Pinkham Notch, NH, 03581, (603) 466-2725. This lodge has many other maps and books about the White Mountains.

Finding the trail: Turn left on the Kancamagus Highway (NH 112) 5 miles east of its junction with I-93, at a large sign: "White Mountain National Forest/ Pemigewasset Wilderness."

Crossing the Pemigewasset River. Wilderness Trail, Lincoln, New Hampshire.

Sources of additional information:

White Mountain National Forest
P.O. Box 638
Laconia, New Hampshire 03247
(603) 528-8721

Loon Mountain Bike Center
Loon Mountain, Kancamagus Highway
Lincoln, New Hampshire 03251
(603) 745-8111, ext. 5566
This private ski resort has a mountain bike shop that offers repairs, rentals, information, and maps. It also opens its trails to biking.

Notes on the trail: Begin on the left side of the parking lot, near an information booth. To do a loop ride, take the road on the right side of the bridge (East Branch Road). It climbs gently on loose gravel, grass, and sand for 3 miles, following the river. When you reach a gate, turn left down to the shore. You will see a line of boulders across the river. Carry your bike on them and onto an island in the river. Take a short path across the island, cross a small stream, and lift your bike up a short, steep embankment. Turn left across a wooden bridge and head back down the Wilderness Trail.

As a side trip, at the bridge, turn right and follow signs for Franconia Falls, three-tenths of a mile farther along a heavily rooted trail. Although biking on the Franconia Falls trail is not forbidden, you might want to stash your bike at the bridge and walk. The trail, which becomes matted with roots, is popular with hikers and walkers, and there's no good place to park your bike near the falls except in the woods.

NOTE: *Mountain Biking in the White Mountain National Forest.* The White Mountains are open to mountain biking with a few restrictions. Riding on the popular Appalachian Trail is forbidden and bikes aren't allowed in 4 large wilderness areas throughout the forest. Otherwise, you can ride almost anywhere, although many trails are too steep and rugged for biking. Wherever you ride, it is important to give hikers a wide berth and be careful not to damage trails.

Five ranger stations in the forest stock maps and information. They are located in the towns of Plymouth, Bethlehem, Gorham, Conway, and one in Bethel, Maine. The main office: White Mountain National Forest, P.O. Box 638, Laconia, NH, 03247, (603) 528-8721. Another important organization in the White Mountains National Forest is the Appalachian Mountain Club (AMC), which is based at the Pinkham Notch Camp (P.O. Box 298, Pinkham Notch, NH, 03581, (603) 466-2725) on NH 16, 18 miles north of the Kancamagus Highway.

RIDE 48 *SAWYER RIVER TRAIL / SAWYER POND TRAIL*

This difficult ride tackles two connected trails in the White Mountains. They're fun and rideable, but a few stretches on these secluded paths will challenge even advanced riders. Also, you must watch for signs at several junctions to stay on the right trail, especially around Sawyer Pond. The ride is made up of an old logging road for several miles, six miles of single-track trails that require short portages across water, boulders, roots, and other minor obstructions, and a return trip (optional) on a scenic highway for five miles.

You're in the heart of the White Mountains, passing through marshy woods and grassland, across a lively river on a narrow bridge, through secluded woods, and along a large, isolated pond. The first several miles of the ride can be done as a moderate out-and-back ride. Along the return trip on the scenic Kancamagus Highway, there is an overlook with a picnic area. Or else you might want to drop off a second vehicle where the ride comes out on the "Kanc" (rhymes with "crank") and skip the last five-mile return stretch on pavement.

General location: On the Kancamagus Highway (NH 112), about 17 miles east of its junction with Interstate 93.
Elevation change: The ride begins at 2,000', climbs gently, and then steeply, for

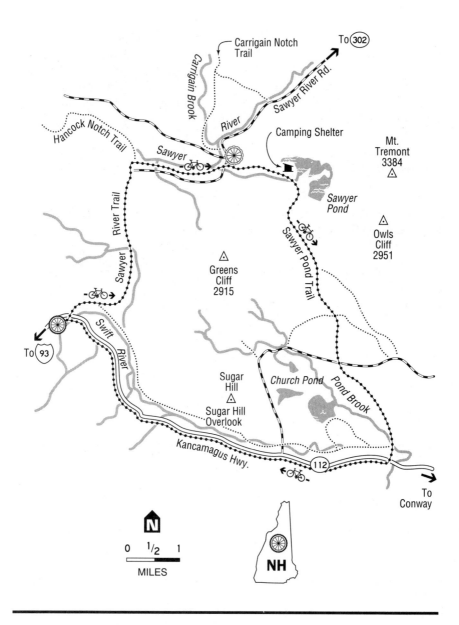

Single-track riding in the White Mountains. Livermore, New Hampshire.

a mile or two to 2,500'. Then you descend more gradually to pavement at 1,250'. Finally, it's a steady 5-mile climb on the Kancamagus Highway. Total elevation gain: 1,750'.

Season: Any time between mid-June and the fall is good for riding.

Services: All services are available on the Kancamagus Highway, especially westward toward Lincoln. Camping is permitted at designated tent sites and cabins in the White Mountains. Repairs and equipment are available at the Loon Mountain Bike Center, Loon Mountain, Kancamagus Highway, Lincoln, (603) 745-8111.

Hazards: Allow plenty of time for completing this ride, since obstructions will slow you. Ride with concentration in the narrower, steeper places. Also, watch for several signs along the trail, to make the all-important connection between the Sawyer River Trail and Sawyer Pond Trail.

Rescue index: You will be as many as 8 miles from assistance. Be prepared to get yourself and your bike back to the trailhead. Pack tools and first-aid supplies on all rides, and know how to use them.

Land status: White Mountain National Forest trails.

Maps: USGS, Mt. Osceola, NH (1967). Also, the "Trail Map & Guide to the White Mountain National Forest" (DeLorme Publishing Company, Box 298, Freeport, ME, 04032) is available in many stores, including the Appalachian Mountain Club (AMC) main lodge on the Kancamagus Highway: Pinkham Notch Camp, P.O. Box 298, Pinkham Notch, NH, 03581, (603) 466-2725. This lodge has many maps and books on the White Mountains.

Finding the trail: The trailhead is at a small turn off on the Kancamagus Highway, about 17 miles east of the junction with I-93.

Sources of additional information:

Loon Mountain Bike Center
Loon Mountain, Kancamagus Highway
Lincoln, New Hampshire 03251
(603) 745-8111
This ski resort has a large mountain bike shop that offers repairs, rentals, information, and maps. The resort also allows mountain biking on its ski trails.

White Mountain National Forest
P.O. Box 638
Laconia, New Hampshire 03247
(603) 528-8721

Appalachian Mountain Club
Pinkham Notch Camp
P.O. Box 298
Pinkham Notch, New Hampshire 03581
(603) 466-2725

Notes on the trail: For those not used to riding on single-track trails through deep woods, these 2 trails, at times, may seem ill-defined. Actually, they're marked at several intersections, and you will pass a couple of helpful maps on trees. You begin riding on the Sawyer River Trail, a single-track path that was once a logging railroad (as a few remaining wooden ties will attest). You soon pass a swimming hole with a waterfall and many boulders for sunbathing. At seven-tenths of a mile you reach an intersection with a wider road. (For an easier out-and-back ride, turn right on this wide, flat trail and head northeast for about 4 miles to NH 302 in Bartlett.) Go straight across this road; you will soon reach a gravel road where you must turn left to cross a large wooden bridge on the Sawyer River. Then go over a footbridge on the right with a sign: "Sawyer Pond Trail." Head up a short, steep path that becomes a challenging trail.

About 5 miles from the trailhead there is a map on a tree on the right. Soon afterward you will reach a fork with a sign on it pointing to shelters to the left and tent platforms to the right. To visit the tranquil, isolated Sawyer Pond, go left. Then backtrack and take the trail to the right on the path marked: "Tent platforms." You will pass along the right side of the pond, with a good view of bare Eagle Cliffs.

Then the trail becomes less distinct as it goes through an older forest. But it soon becomes clearer and reaches an intersection. Cross the intersection and about a mile later, after riding downhill, cross a logging road. You will pass a sign: "Kancamagus Highway, 1.5 miles." Continue along this grassy trail until it comes out on the highway (known as "the Kanc," rhymes with "crank"). Turn right to ride back to the trailhead. This is a highway, but most local motorists are used to bicyclists.

RIDE 49 *DOUBLEHEAD*

This challenging 16-mile loop ride has a bit of everything in it: steady climbing on secluded forest roads, more climbing on grassy double-track trails to a scenic clearing, descents on single- and double-track trails, and easy rolling through the countryside on dirt and paved roads. About half of the ride uses gravel and dirt roads, four miles are on trails, and four miles on pavement. Half of the ride is uphill.

The ride begins on an access road through the 750,000-acre White Mountain National Forest. These are unusual byways: immaculately maintained dirt roads meant to be temporary, built mainly for logging and other forest maintenance purposes. Next, you fork onto a grassy trail that climbs to a highland clearing. Once back in light woods, it's a rolling descent to a pastoral landscape of attractive houses and fields, with more views. To reach the trailhead, you ride up a scenic road along the East Branch of the Saco River, with a swimming hole in it a half mile from NH 16.

General location: Jackson, 4 miles north of North Conway, off NH 16.
Elevation change: You will gain about 1,400' on this ride. It climbs steadily for about 6 miles on dirt roads, with several short, steep descents on trails and dirt roads.
Season: Any time between mid-June and fall is good for riding. It helps to ask local riders about current trail conditions.
Services: All services are available in recreation-oriented North Conway and Conway along NH 16. The Mt. Washington Valley region is known for its year-round recreational services. Jackson has some good restaurants, too.
Hazards: Be ready for several steep descents on single-track trails and hard-packed dirt roads, with a few water bars on the trails and oncoming traffic on the dirt roads. Make sure your brakes are working well.
Rescue index: You can be as far as 8 miles from assistance in this secluded forest.
Land status: National forest roads and trails and active town roads.

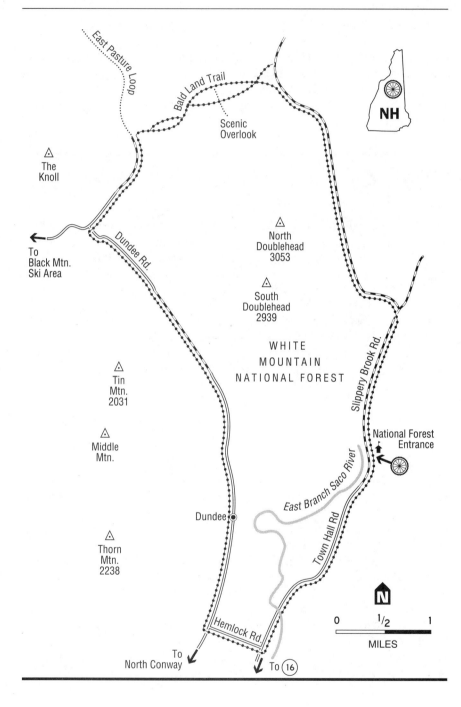

East Pasture Loop

Bald Land Trail

Scenic
Overlook

The
Knoll

To
Black Mtn.
Ski Area

Dundee Rd.

North
Doublehead
3053

South
Doublehead
2939

WHITE
MOUNTAIN
NATIONAL FOREST

Slippery Brook Rd.

Tin
Mtn.
2031

Middle
Mtn.

National Forest
Entrance

East Branch Saco River

Dundee

Town Hall Rd

Thorn
Mtn.
2238

NH

N

Hemlock Rd.

To
North Conway

To 16

0   1/2   1

MILES

A highland clearing of new growth. Jackson, New Hampshire.

Maps: USGS, Jackson, NH. The Mountain Cycle Guide Service in Intervale, (603) 383-9405, has developed a map of about 20 rides in the Mt. Washington Valley area; it is available for a small fee.

Finding the trail: Take Town Hall Road north off NH 16, 1.5 miles south of the junction of NH 16 and NH 302. Drive east, following the East Branch Saco River on the right. Fork left at about 3 miles on unpaved Slippery Brook Road. After another eight-tenths of a mile you will reach a sign ("White Mountain National Forest"), a gate, and parking areas on either side of the road just before the gate. Or you might have a friend drop you off here, do the same loop, and finish by riding down to NH 302.

Sources of additional information: The Mountain Cycle Guide Service in Intervale, (603) 383-9405, has a map of more than 20 rides in the Mt. Washington Valley area. It also offers instruction and advice. The Joe Jones Ski and Sports on Main Street in North Conway, (603) 356-9411, is a full-service mountain bike shop that also rents bikes.

Notes on the trail: Ride up the road from the entrance gate for about 2 miles and turn left. Climb another 2.5 miles, until you cross a bridge and pass a logged area with views on the left. You will reach a left fork onto a grassy trail. (If you miss the fork you soon come to the end of the road.) The trail begins with a short, steep climb. After about six-tenths of a mile, on a third short climb, turn left at a marker on a tree about 20 feet away that reads "Bald Land Trail." Climb on this fast, smooth, grassy trail, staying to the left at a small fork after about three-tenths of a mile, and immediately afterward reaching a right turn marked "East Pasture Loop to Jackson." This is the highest point on the ride. Before going downhill to the right you might take a short, scenic side trip. Go straight into a clearing, riding through new growth onto a path at the other side and into another clearing, where there are excellent views of mountain ranges to the west.

Return to the trail marked "East Pasture Loop to Jackson," and prepare your bike and yourself for a steep downhill. After the descent, take a left fork on a grassy single-track trail, staying to the left and going through an intersection. Cross a wooden bridge and take another left. The path becomes loose gravel. Stay to the left and go through another intersection. The trail now becomes a town road, leaving the woods and becoming paved, and goes steeply downhill to an intersection with a stone house on the left. Turn left up paved Dundee Road; you'll climb a bit and then go downhill on dirt. After several miles you will pass a condominium complex on the right, with a view behind it. Turn right on the next road, Hemlock Road (marked with a street sign facing the other direction). Bear right on Vista Lane, and come out on Town Hall Road, about 2 miles below the trailhead.

RIDE 50 *CHERRY MOUNTAIN / JEFFERSON NOTCH*

Be ready to climb for about 9 miles on dirt roads on this challenging 27-mile loop through the White Mountain National Forest. Panoramic views make it worth the effort. From Cherry Mountain Road you pass vistas of the northern Presidentials—Mt. Madison, Mt. Jefferson, Mt. Adams, Mt. Sam Adams, and Mt. Quincy Adams. More excellent views come at the northern end of this road. The ride returns on the state's highest public road, Jefferson Notch Road (it's closed in the winter), and then along scenic Jefferson Brook. Near the beginning and end of the ride are two falls, Lower and Upper Ammonoosuc Falls. The ride includes about six miles of pavement.

More hiking and snowmobiling trails are south of this ride, in Bethlehem, Franconia, and Lincoln, as well as east of Jefferson Notch Road. Lower Ammonoosuc Falls, one-quarter mile from the parking lot, is a swimming hole. Jefferson Brook is also swimmable.

General location: On US 302, 20 miles east of Littleton.
Elevation change: The ride gains a total of 2,500'. It begins with a steady, not-too-steep climb of about 650' for 3.5 miles, and then levels off. The second half of the ride is a steeper 1,600' climb for 3.5 miles to Jefferson Notch (3,008'), and a 4.5-mile descent.

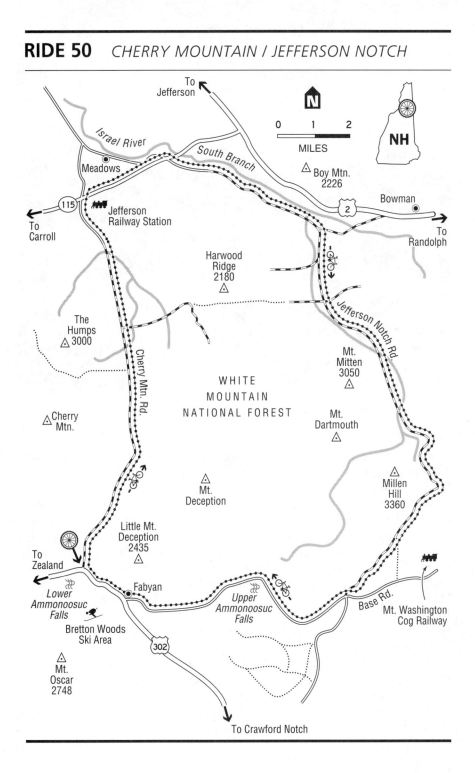

Mountain bike shop at Loon Mountain. Lincoln, New Hampshire.

Season: You can do this ride from about mid-June through fall. Jefferson Notch Road is closed for the winter until May.

Services: Bring plenty of water, since it's not easily available without detouring. At the northern end of the ride, 2 miles east on US 2, there is the historic Lowe store, which carries almost everything. There's also a general store in Fabyan, across from the Bretton Woods Ski Area, where the ride comes out on US 302. Camping areas dot the region, including at Zealand on US 302, 2 miles west of the trailhead, and further along US 302. There are bike shops in North Conway, 20 miles to the southeast, and Littleton, 20 miles west.

Hazards: Watch out for oncoming traffic when descending onto Jefferson Notch Road.

Rescue index: You are about 5 miles from assistance at the farthest.

Land status: Town and state roads.

Maps: USGS, Mt. Washington, 1982. The Mountain Cycle Guide Service in Intervale, (603) 383-9405, has developed a map of more than 20 rides in the Mt. Washington Valley area; it is available for a small fee.

Finding the trail: From the south, drive north and west from Crawford Notch on US 302. Go 1 mile beyond the Fabyan store on the right. Turn onto Cherry Mountain Road and immediately left into the parking area for Lower Ammonoosuc Falls.

Sources of additional information: The Mountain Cycle Guide Service in Intervale, (603) 383-9405, has a map of more than 20 rides in the Mt. Washington Valley area. It also offers instruction and advice. The Joe Jones Ski and Sports on Main Street in North Conway, (603) 356-9411, is a full-service mountain bike shop.

Notes on the trail: From the parking area at Lower Ammonoosuc Falls, turn northward on Cherry Mountain Road, which climbs for 3.4 miles. Then descend 3.5 miles to NH 115. Turn right on NH 115 and ride for about 2 miles. Cross the railroad tracks and continue until you reach the junction with the loosely graveled Valley Road. Turn right and travel on Valley Road for about 3 miles, along the Israel River, until you reach the junction on the right with Jefferson Notch Road. Turn right and climb again, gently for 2 miles, then steeply for 3.5 miles (with occasional easier stretches). From Jefferson Notch descend steeply along Jefferson Brook for 3.5 miles to the junction with Base Road. Turn right and descend on pavement for 4.5 miles back to the Fabyan store on US 302. Turn right and return to Lower Ammonoosuc Falls.

RIDE 51 _CASCADE FALLS_

Ride for a mile or two, or all the way to a neighboring town, on the out-and-back old road and rugged trail along a wide river. You can head either north or south for four miles from Gorham, through new-growth clearings and light woods. After about 2.5 miles to the north, toward Berlin and modest Cascade Falls, this ride becomes difficult because of loose rocks and short climbs. To the south it's much gentler, paralleling more closely the Androscoggin River. This ride can be linked with the Leadmine Ledge ride.

General location: Just outside Gorham.

Elevation change: The terrain is relatively flat, but has some technical climbing on cobbly, broken ground to the north.

Season: Any time between mid-June and winter is good for riding. Snowmobilers pack the trails in winter.

Services: All services are available in Gorham, including Moriah Sports bike shop, 101 Main Street, (603) 466-5050.

Hazards: Although the route is flat, expect loose terrain to the north.

Rescue index: You will be about 1 mile from assistance.

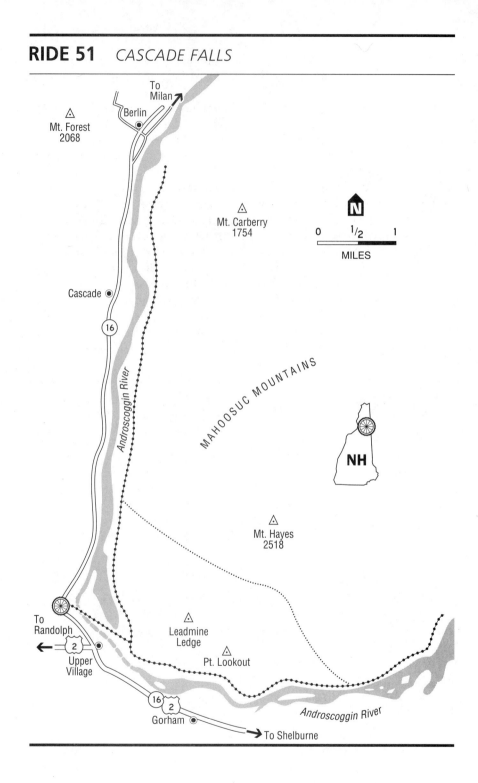

To Milan

Berlin

△ Mt. Forest
2068

△ Mt. Carberry
1754

N

0   1/2   1

MILES

Cascade ◉

16

Androscoggin River

MAHOOSUC MOUNTAINS

NH

△ Mt. Hayes
2518

To Randolph

2

Upper Village

△ Leadmine Ledge

△ Pt. Lookout

16

2

Gorham ◉

Androscoggin River

To Shelburne

Land status: An old town road and former railroad bed.

Maps: USGS, Berlin, NH (1970). Moriah Sports in Gorham also has maps of local rides.

Finding the trail: From NH 16 go through Gorham on Main Street, then continue on NH 16 north at its intersection with NH 2. Just after the intersection you'll reach a large railroad bridge. Park in the gravel lot on the right beneath the bridge.

Sources of additional information: Moriah Sports in Gorham, 101 Main Street, (603) 466-5050, is a complete mountain bike shop. They offer rentals, repairs, tours, maps, and plain old good advice.

Notes on the trail: Head north on NH 16 just a few hundred feet beyond the bridge, and turn right down a short, paved access road to the riverbed. If there is no water and you get up enough momentum, it's a fun, safe ride across the bed of loose rocks. On the other side of the river turn right onto a dirt road. After eight-tenths of a mile you will reach an uphill left fork. Turn left and then immediately right, and ride over an old brick dam. On the other side, turn either left or right on the old road.

To the left (north) the ride becomes much more rugged after about 2.5 miles, heading toward Berlin and the Cascade Falls. It is rolling terrain with some small water crossings. Turn right for a smoother and flatter ride toward Shelbourne. After 2 miles to the right you will reach a clearing with a road forking uphill to the left. Veer right to continue on this ride. You would turn left to do the Leadmine Ledge ride.

RIDE 52 *LEADMINE LEDGE*

This moderately challenging 7.5-mile loop ride bounces along a river for a mile or two, before climbing into woods with popular hiking trails. Then it descends steeply onto a single-track trail to a jeep trail along the river, linking up with the Cascade Falls ride. About half of this loop uses four-wheel-drive roads, 2.5 miles is on double-track trails, and about one mile is on a single-track trail.

The ride first crosses an almost dry river channel, and then a handsome old brick dam. After taking in views to the south along the river, you will climb through deep woods to a highland trail with small brooks across it. On this ridge you can scout out panoramic views on the left. After you descend, the landscape changes to clearings of new growth.

General location: Just outside Gorham.

Elevation change: The ride gains 900'. After cruising along a river for a couple of miles it climbs steadily and not too steeply, and then descends.

Season: Any time between mid-June and winter is good for riding. Ask about current trail conditions at Moriah Sports bike shop in Gorham.

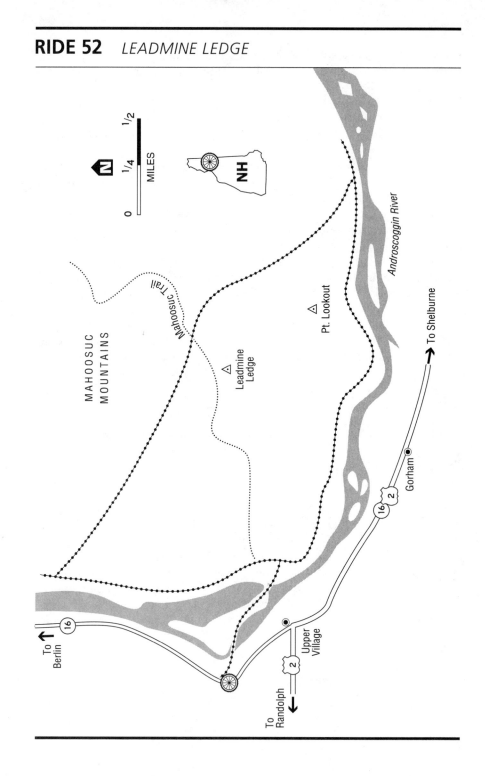

Services: All services are available in Gorham. The bike shop is Moriah Sports at 101 Main Street in Gorham, (603) 466-5050.

Hazards: When you get to the height-of-land you'll find the trail rougher and occasionally obstructed by a fallen branch. The downhill is quite steep in stretches and can be obstructed—be ready to crouch and brake.

Rescue index: At the farthest, you are about 2 miles from assistance on a secluded trail.

Land status: An old town road, logging road, power line road, and abandoned all-terrain vehicle trail.

Maps: Maps of this and other local rides are available at Moriah Sports in Gorham.

Finding the trail: From NH 16, go through Gorham on Main Street and continue on NH 16 north at its intersection with NH 2. Just after the intersection you reach a large railroad bridge. Park in the gravel lot on the right beneath the bridge.

Sources of additional information: Moriah Sports at 101 Main Street in Gorham, (603) 466-5050, is a complete mountain bike shop offering rentals, repairs, tours, maps, and plain old good advice.

Notes on the trail: Head north on NH 16 for a few hundred feet beyond the bridge and turn right down a short, paved access road to the riverbed. If there's no water in the riverbed, and you get up enough momentum, it's a fun, safe ride across the bed of loose rocks. On the other side turn right onto a dirt road. After eight-tenths of a mile you reach an uphill left fork. Turn left and immediately right, and ride over an old brick dam. Turn right on an old road that parallels the Androscoggin River. Turn right downhill and into the woods. After 2 miles you reach a clearing with a broad road forking uphill to the left.

Turn left and go uphill on this loose gravel road for a short distance. Fork left on a smooth, grassy trail into the woods. After about 2 miles you will climb a rocky, eroded stretch of trail. You might notice the blue blazes on trees on either side of the trail along this stretch. The popular Mahoosuc hiking trail crosses the trail here. But don't ride on it. Instead, one-third of a mile after crossing a stream, while going downhill, look for a soft left fork onto a narrower trail. Turn onto this single-track trail and descend. Then veer left at a small clearing with an old campsite. After 1 mile the trail will come out on a power line road next to the river. Turn left and ride back to the dam. Or turn right and ride on this progressively more challenging road (see the Cascade Falls ride).

MAINE

RIDE 53 MOUNT AGAMENTICUS

This southernmost mountain biking area in Maine has many miles of trails including the eight-mile loop described here. Most of the loop follows moderately technical double- and single-track trails through secluded woods, with about a mile on two-wheel-drive dirt roads. (There is an easier loop that connects with this one just to the west.) Except for a short stretch at the beginning and end of this ride on a dirt road, you're in deep woods. Like all forests, though, this is more than trees. Besides stands of hardwoods and softwoods you will pass a large pond, a swamp, several brooks, and stone walls.

You can also ride or drive up the steep, paved access road at the beginning of the ride to the summit of Mt. Agamenticus, where you can climb a fire tower for a panoramic view or relax on a clearing. Then you might descend on a short, steep trail at the northern edge of the parking lot, which veers left and comes out on the access road after eight-tenths of a mile. Four miles north of the ride is Maine's most popular ocean beach, Ogunquit Beach.

General location: York, 4 miles west of Interstate 95.

Elevation change: This ride is on relatively flat terrain, with short climbs and descents.

Season: Riding is good from June through winter, with some wetness during the spring.

Services: All services are available along US 1. Bicycle Bob's Bicycle Outlet at 990 Lafayette Road, Portsmouth, New Hampshire 03801, (603) 431-3040, is a full service mountain bike shop.

Hazards: At times these secluded trails can be tricky to follow, especially in autumn when leaves cover tracks. But the area is compact and bounded on all sides by roads; use these to orient yourself. The trails are also used occasionally by hikers, equestrians, and all-terrain vehicles.

Rescue index: You will be about 3 miles from assistance at the farthest.

Land status: Old roads and public trails on town water supply land.

Maps: USGS, York Harbor, ME. Not all of the single-track trails on this ride are mapped.

Finding the trail: From the south, take the last exit before the toll on Interstate 95 at York Village. Head north on US 1 for 3.5 miles (a half mile past the junction with US 1A), Turn left onto Mountain Road, following it for 4 miles and watching so that you don't fork onto smaller roads. After about 3 miles, fork left onto Agamenticus Road. Just before the road becomes dirt there is a turnoff on the right. You can park here, or turn right and climb the pavement to a parking lot at Mt. Agamenticus.

Sources of additional information: A group ride often meets at the base of Mt. Agamenticus on weekend mornings. Also, there's Bicycle Bob's Bicycle Outlet, address and phone number above.

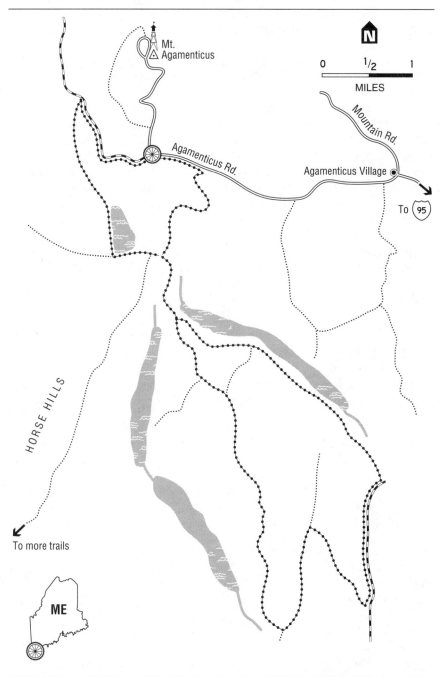

N

0   1/2   1
MILES

Mountain Rd.

Mt.
△ Agamenticus

Agamenticus Rd.

Agamenticus Village

To 95

HORSE HILLS

To more trails

ME

Notes on the trail: Begin riding westward on the unpaved Agamenticus Road. At the first four-wheel-drive road turn left sharply and head downhill. (This turn appears approximately a half mile into the ride.) In a tenth of a mile or so fork left onto a double-track trail. A mile later you will pass a pond on the left. The trail may become harder to follow. Keep going straight (southeast), veering left at the next trail junction and passing a reservoir on the right.

Soon you will cross the (considerably wider) main north/south trail. Turning left here takes you back to Agamenticus Road, for a short loop. Or turn right onto a single-track trail going uphill. At the next intersection (with a pond on the right) turn left, then take the next left uphill. This scenic single-track trail follows along a large pond, becomes wider and grassier, and veers to the right uphill. Watch for a sharp, distinct right turn onto a double-track trail. Take this turn; you are now heading northward. (If you miss this turn you will soon reach a paved road.) When you reach a small clearing ride through it, then bear to the left.

At the next three trail junctions turn right each time. Then veer right at the reservoir (visible through the trees); you're now on the same trail you rode south on. You soon will reach the main trail junction again. Turn right on the trail; you will reach paved Agamenticus Road. Turn left and ride back to the access road for Mt. Agamenticus.

RIDE 54 *ATHERTON HILL*

This moderate 3.5-mile loop lies at the center of a network of snowmobile trails and is intersected by a long rideable power line. You begin and end on a four-wheel-drive road. The rest of the ride follows well-worn trails with occasional water and mud, and a short, steep, eroded descent.

From a fire tower on Atherton Hill you have a 360-degree view of the countryside, including the huge Forest Lake to the east. The rest of the time you will roll through pleasant woods with sunny clearings where you can snack on blackberries in late summer.

General location: Windam, 10 miles northwest of Portland.
Elevation change: It is a steady, not-too-steep climb of about 300′ to the fire tower.
Season: You can begin riding here in about June. Local mountain bikers also use these trails during the winter, once they (the trails) are packed down by snowmobilers. The only good thing about the racket made by snowmobiles is that they'll never surprise you around a bend.
Services: All services are available in North Windham and along US 302. There is a good private campground on Little Sebago Lake.

RIDE 54   *ATHERTON HILL*

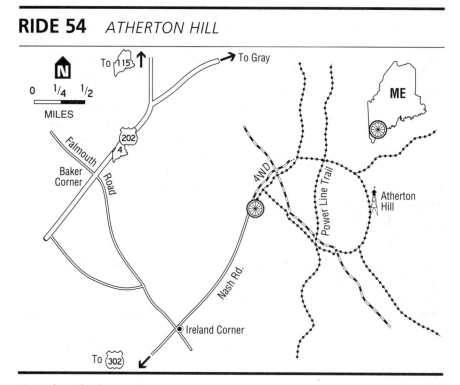

Hazards: The descent from Atherton Hill has a short, steep, eroded section that beginners should not attempt.

Rescue index: You are never more than a mile from assistance.

Land status: Town road and snowmobile trails with year-round access.

Maps: USGS, Gorham, ME.

Finding the trail: From Portland take US 302 west for about 9 miles. Just before the junction with ME 4 turn right on the paved Nash Road, following it for 2 miles through an intersection until it becomes unpaved. Park along the road—away from any homes. From Interstate 495 take Exit 11 in Gray; get on US 202/ ME 4 heading south. Turn left at the first intersection after the junction with ME 115, then left after 1 mile onto Nash Road.

Sources of additional information: Back Bay Bicycle at 333 Forest Avenue in Portland, (207) 773-6906, has weekly mountain bike rides and information about riding areas. Another shop is Cyclemania at 59 Federal Street in Portland, (207) 774-2933.

Notes on the trail: Head up Nash Road past a large, rusted "no trespassing" sign that does not apply to bicyclists heading toward Atherton Hill. After three-tenths of a mile you pass a road on the right—this is where you'll come out at ride's end. Keep going straight through a 4-way intersection, and fork right in the woods. Fork right again after one-third mile, and right again after eight-tenths of a mile. You will reach the power line—another favorite ride in the Portland area. It begins at Babbidge Road to the south and goes north for several miles. Fork right on the trail just before reaching the power line, cross the power line, and pick up a trail on the other side. (If the trail is overgrown after crossing the power line, you took another trail just to the left of the correct trail.) You will reach a fire tower in a clearing.

The trail continues on the other side of the fire tower. At the next fork, which comes in about 1.5 miles, fork right. Then turn right on a wider trail. You will cross the power line again. Then veer left and come out on Nash Road. Turn left and ride back down Nash Road.

RIDE 55 *MICA MINES*

This four-mile loop passes a couple of abandoned mica quarries, which later became part of a town park. Today the park is owned by the local National Guard, which uses it only occasionally. There is some technical riding on double-track trails, over roots and rocks. You can explore the quarries—two large holes—

RIDE 55 *MICA MINES*

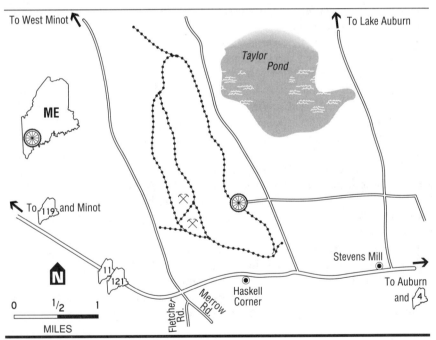

A rugged old mining road. Auburn, Maine.

and you might meet a local prospector there looking for a nugget of greenish tourmaline.

General location: Just west of Lewiston and Auburn.

Elevation change: The terrain is relatively flat with regular short climbs and descents.

Season: The best time to ride here is between mid-June and fall.

Services: All services are available on ME 121, in Auburn, and in Lewiston. Two nearby bike shops are the Twin City Cyclery at 199 Bartlett Street in Lewiston, (207) 783-0622, and the Moe Bike shop in Lewiston, (207) 783-2641.

Hazards: None except for minor obstructions on the trails. On occasion the National Guard holds maneuvers here, in which case it may be wise to forgo the riding.

Rescue index: Houses and roads border the park.

Land status: This abandoned town park is now managed by the National Guard. The town swapped the land for an adjoining clearing that is now a baseball field.

Maps: There is no map of this park, but the area is compact enough that you can't get lost. In fact, you might want to explore side trails that come out on surrounding roads. The public library in Auburn has some historical information about the mines.

Finding the trail: From ME 4 in Auburn and Lewiston take ME 11/ME 121 for about 2 miles. Turn right at signs for the Lost Valley Ski Area and Lake Auburn, and then turn left on Stephen Mills Road. This road ends at the entrance to both the Auburn Suburban Little League field and the National Guard site. Park across from the baseball field.

Sources of additional information: Try L.L. Bean on Route 1 in Freeport, (207) 865-3161. This famous mail-order house has a bike shop in the basement. The clerks will discuss this and other rides.

Notes on the trail: This is a counterclockwise loop. Ride north away from the baseball field and National Guard building, across a sandy area, until you reach a mounded trailhead into the woods. The first fork in the trail comes in four-tenths of a mile; veer left. You are climbing on a single-track trail. Take the next left and you will reach a secluded clearing. Turn left at a "T" junction and keep bearing left on the main trail. You will reach an abandoned quarry with bits of glittering mica covering the trail like fallen stars. Turn left, then veer left on a sandy road that goes downhill toward the National Guard building. To extend this ride and pass another quarry turn right at the last junction, onto a sandy road, and climb. Then fork right and loop back to the same trail you came up on. Just before coming out of the woods, turn left on a trail and ride into the sandy lot near the baseball field.

RIDE 56 *HEBRON-BUCKFIELD RAIL TRAIL*

This easy 9-mile (round-trip) out-and-back ride follows a flat, rural, scenic trail that was once a railroad bed. Today the route is a well-maintained, hard-packed gravel and dirt path. It is a good ride for new mountain bikers, youths, and families, as well as cyclists who want to crank along at a fast pace. For railroad travelers half the fun must have been getting there on this line, which runs through a pleasant landscape of light woods, open fields, and active farms, crossing several wooden bridges along the way.

General location: Between Hebron and Buckfield, and extending north into Sumner, 10 miles northwest of Lewiston.

Elevation change: Flat.

Season: This trail can be ridden in all 4 seasons. It has good drainage in the spring, shade in the summer, views in the fall, and a snowmobile-packed surface in the winter.

Services: There is a country store in West Minot and several country stores in Buckfield. At the junction of ME 124 and the trail you can camp at a campground.

Hazards: None.

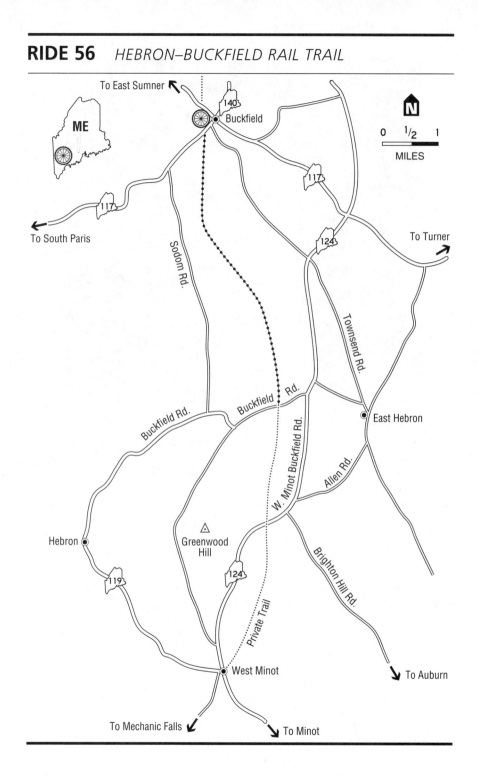

Cruise or crank on a flat trail. Buckfield, Maine.

Rescue index: You are always close to farms and roads.
Land status: An abandoned railroad bed.
Maps: *The Maine Atlas and Gazetteer* (DeLorme Mapping Co., Freeport, ME) is a collection of detailed non-topographical maps available in many stores.
Finding the trail: From its terminus in Buckfield, the rail trail begins off ME 117, just south of the junction with ME 140, on the left next to a dirt road in an industrial lot.

Sources of additional information:

The Rails-to-Trails Conservancy
1400 16th Street, NW
Washington, D.C. 200326
(202) 797-5400
This is a national clearinghouse for rail trails.

The Buckfield Mall, a country store in Buckfield.
(207) 336-2659

Notes on the trail: You can ride on this rail trail at least 3 miles farther north from Buckfield. Pick it up again at the top of a road that forks to the left off ME 140, just northwest of Buckfield. The trail begins on the right side of the road.

RIDE 57 *PLEASANT MOUNTAIN*

This moderate 4.5-mile loop, with an optional four-mile out-and-back stretch, progresses from sparsely inhabited rural countryside to a secluded clearing with a spectacular 180-degree view of the surrounding countryside. You begin on a dirt road that becomes more and more rugged. The rest of the ride uses double- and single-track trails, except for the return stretch on a dirt road. The optional out-and-back ride is a more challenging descent and ascent, on loose rock in places.

The view from the height-of-land takes in Meadow Mountain to the north-

RIDE 57 *PLEASANT MOUNTAIN*

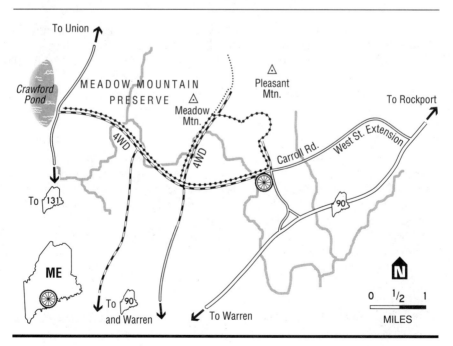

A steep trail past blueberry bushes. West Rockport, Maine.

west. While enjoying the scenery, you can sample the blueberries in late summer. (*However,* look first for a sign—where the trail enters the field—that advises against eating blueberries if there's been a recent spraying.) Just west of this ride is recreational Crawford Pond, with swimming and camping. Four miles eastward lies the popular seacoast city of Camden, with many shops, restaurants, and ocean views. This can be a good companion ride to the Hope ride, ten miles to the north.

General location: West Rockport, 4.5 miles west of Rockport.
Elevation change: The ride begins at 280', climbs gradually to 335', then steeply to 515'. The out-and-back trail descends from 335' to 120'.
Season: Any time from June through the winter is fine for riding. Snowmobilers pack down the trails in the winter.
Services: All services are available in Rockport and Camden.
Hazards: There is a somewhat steep descent on the second half of the ride that requires technical skill.
Rescue index: You are about 2 miles from assistance at the farthest.
Land status: Old town roads.
Maps: *The Maine Atlas and Gazetteer* (DeLorme Mapping Co., Freeport, ME) is a collection of detailed road maps available in many stores.

Finding the trail: From US 1 turn onto ME 90. After 2.5 miles you will pass through the intersection with ME 17, heading toward Warren. After another half mile turn right onto West St. Extension, then fork left after a half mile and reach the intersection of two dirt roads. Park off the left side of the road, just after the intersection.

Sources of additional information: Maine Sport Outfitters on Route 1 in Rockport, (207) 236-7120, is a large sporting goods store with a mountain biking department.

Notes on the trail: Continue riding down the access road, which soon turns to dirt and gravel and then a more rugged surface. The loop turns right onto Mountain Road. But ahead is a fun, somewhat challenging 2-mile out-and-back ride on a rocky and grassy trail, which comes out on a paved road near recreational Crawford Pond. Then double back to the junction.

After turning onto Mountain Road descend for a while, then climb on rock, and cross a power line. Now comes a slightly tricky turn: 1.5 miles after turning onto Mountain Road take a sharp, steep right turn uphill through a clearing of blueberry bushes. Climb on this steep, short path, and stop at the top to enjoy the panoramic view. Then descend into the woods and reach a "T" junction. Turn left and pick up a two-wheel-drive dirt road that comes out at the intersection where you began.

RIDE 58 *HOPE*

This moderate four-mile loop begins in high farm country, entering secluded woods and coming out again in an open field with good views of distant mountains. There are about 2.5 miles of rugged double-track trails, a mile on a jeep road, and a half mile on a paved rural road. This is a good companion ride to the Pleasant Mountain ride, ten miles south of it.

Before heading off, though, take in the panoramic view of Moody Mountain to the northeast. Then, after about 1.5 miles on two dirt roads, ride for a short distance past the second left turn into a bright clearing, where you can find thorny blackberry bushes with their sweet, seedy fruits in early fall.

General location: Town of Hope.

Elevation change: You begin riding at 600', descend to 270', and climb again to 600', for a total gain of 660'.

Season: Riding is best anytime from late June through fall. Snowmobilers pack down the trails in the winter.

Services: All services are available in Hope and Camden. Camden is a scenic seaside town 9 miles away, and well worth a visit.

RIDE 58   *HOPE*

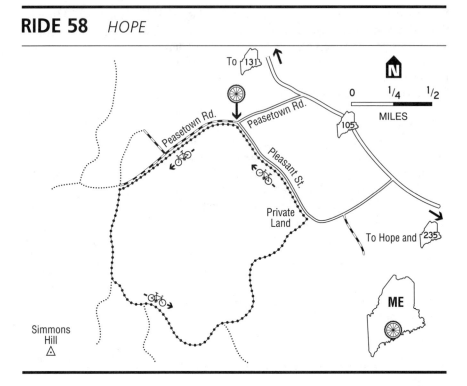

Hazards: Watch for the usual minor obstructions on the narrower stretches of the trail.

Rescue index: You will be about 2 miles from assistance at the farthest.

Land status: Old roads and a snowmobile trail through woods and fields with riding permission granted to mountain bikers.

Maps: *The Maine Atlas and Gazetteer* (DeLorme Mapping Co., Freeport, Maine) shows all of this ride except the middle section, which is blazed.

Finding the trail: On ME 105 west, 2.3 miles northwest of its junction with ME 235 and after a hill, turn left onto Peasetown Road. Park at the top of the hill, when the pavement veers to the right.

Sources of additional information: Maine Sport Outfitters on Route 1 in Rockport, (207) 236-7120, is a large sporting goods store with a mountain biking department.

Notes on the trail: Once you have parked at the top of the hill (off Peasetown Road), pick up the jeep road to the right—opposite the paved Peasetown Road. Stay on the dirt road for eight-tenths of a mile, past a left and right fork. Then turn left onto a wide trail. After four-tenths of a mile turn left onto a narrower trail, about 100 feet before you reach a clearing. This narrower trail may be somewhat overgrown in the summer. Follow it as it climbs and winds through the woods, finally veering to the left. After about 1.5 miles, you come out at a farm

A trailhead with a view. Hope, Maine.

field with a good view of mountains beyond it. Ride across the field—giving a friendly wave and slowing down if there is someone working there—and arrive at a farm on a paved road. (The owners allow mountain bikers to cross their land. This is rural Maine, not Marin County.) Turn left onto the paved road; in a half mile or so you'll be back at the trailhead.

RIDE 59 *OLD COUNTY ROAD*

This convenient 8.5-mile loop begins and ends on US 1, Maine's scenic coastal highway. You climb briefly on a paved road (turn around for a good view of the Atlantic Ocean) and then head into the woods on four-wheel-drive roads and a grassy trail. After reaching a rural community you return to the shore on a trail that turns into a two-wheel-drive dirt road, and cruise along attractive, paved US 1 for the last 1.5 miles.

Although it's not as famous as Bar Harbor or Camden, two other coastal Maine towns, Searsport *is* famous for having raised more sea captains than any other city in the United States. Not surprisingly, it has a maritime museum,

RIDE 59 *OLD COUNTY ROAD*

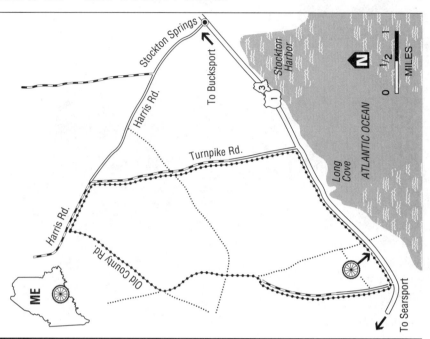

located in a half-dozen buildings (pick up a museum map in town). Many of the large homes where the sea captains lived are now comfortable bed-and-breakfast inns.

General location: Just outside Searsport, 30 miles north of Camden.
Elevation change: The ride begins with a steady climb and ends with a steady descent, both of them modest.
Season: Any time between mid-June and winter is good for riding. Spring can mean mud on the trails. Snowmobilers pack down the trails in winter.
Services: All services are available along US 1 in Searsport and Stockton Springs.
Hazards: There are occasional hidden obstructions on the trails during the late summer, when the underbrush grows taller and thicker.
Rescue index: You will be within 1.5 miles of assistance.
Land status: Town roads, abandoned county roads, and a highway.
Maps: USGS, Searsport, ME. Also, *The Maine Atlas and Gazetteer* (DeLorme Mapping Co., Freeport, ME), a collection of detailed non-topographical maps, is available in many stores.
Finding the trail: You can park at Birgfeld's Bicycle Shop on US 1 in Searsport. From the south the shop is on the left in a small building complex, just across from a large flea market.

Once a road, now a trail. Searsport, Maine.

Sources of additional information: Birgfeld's Bicycle Shop on Rt. 1 in Searsport is a meeting place for all kinds of rides, most of them sponsored by the Free-wheelers, Maine's largest bike touring club. Off-road rides leave from the shop every week. Phone: (207) 548-2916.

Notes on the trail: Head south on US 1 from Birgfeld's Bicycle Shop for a half mile. A right turn onto Black Road is somewhat obscured; it is an unnamed paved road between 2 large overhanging trees just after a downhill. After seven-tenths of a mile this road becomes unpaved, then becomes a trail. Stay to the left and respect the fact that this old road goes through private land, as indicated by "No Trespassing" signs on trees.

After another half mile or so you intersect a pipeline trail. Go straight. (For a longer, wetter ride turn left and loop around on the pipeline trail.) The main trail becomes wet for a few hundred feet. Then stay to the left at a fork, and turn right at the "T" junction. You will reach another "T" junction; turn right and ride for about a half mile on a secluded, grassy single-track trail, coming out on a dirt road past several houses. Continue on this dirt road until it arrives at a "T" junction on a two-wheel-drive dirt road. Turn right and reach a paved road. Turn right again, and after a few hundred feet, fork right on a narrow grassy road. After about a mile this road widens, and after another mile becomes paved. When you reach US 1, turn right.

RIDE 60 *ACADIA NATIONAL PARK*

This highly popular national park has over 50 miles of wide gravel paths that interconnect in easy and moderate loops ranging from 3 to 20 miles. The park is famous for its panoramic views of the Atlantic Ocean, and a network of "carriage roads" (built by millionaire John D. Rockefeller in 1915) is the best way to see them. All of the roads have well-maintained surfaces. The farther you go from a trailhead, however, the narrower, steeper, and grassier they become. Some of the roads can also be a bit sandy, requiring steering and braking skills.

On lower-lying loops you will pass through a maintained landscape of spruce and hemlock woods, granite bridges, brooks, and glacier-formed lakes. But be sure to do a loop or two that climb. Along these panoramic trails you will find blueberries growing on low bushes in sunny spots. There's also swimming at Echo Lake, hiking and camping, and many quaint stores and eateries in Bar Harbor. The Visitor Center at the northern end of the park has a film about the park and a bookstore. To enjoy Acadia and other places on Mt. Desert Island thoroughly, you'll need more than a day. Plan ahead during the extremely busy summer months.

General location: On Mt. Desert Island, near the town of Bar Harbor.
Elevation change: Carriage roads around the lakes are flat, while more secluded ones can climb gradually.
Season: These roads can be ridden in all seasons. In summer the park is very busy.
Services: All services are available in Bar Harbor, 2 miles to the east. Less busy services are available along ME 3 outside Bar Harbor. There is an American Youth Hostel (AYH) in Bar Harbor, (207) 288-5587, open only in July and August.
Hazards: Watch out for other trail users, especially around trailheads and on less challenging loops. Also, watch out for oncoming cyclists and hikers, especially when descending around turns and on sandy terrain.
Rescue index: Carriage roads are well used and are easily accessible. But at times you'll be several miles from a trailhead, and there's no guarantee that another rider will appear. Be prepared.
Land status: National Park roads.
Maps: A map of Mt. Desert Island is available at bike shops in Bar Harbor or by writing to: Superintendent, Acadia National Park, Bar Harbor, ME, 04609.
  "A Pocket Guide to the Carriage Roads of Acadia National Park" (Down East

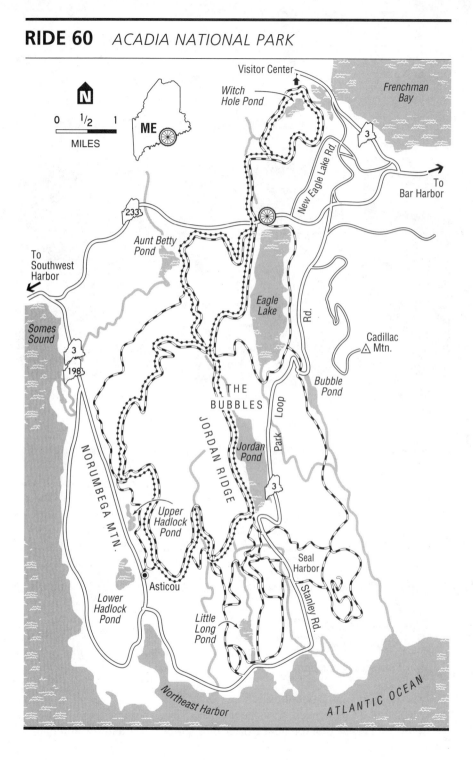

Carriage road with a spectacular view of the Atlantic Ocean. Acadia National Park, Mt. Desert Island, Maine.

Books) has 11 loops in it. It's also available at bookstores and bike shops in Bar Harbor.

Finding the trail: You can pick up the carriage roads at several locations: the Visitor Center at the northern end of the park; Park Loop Road at Bubble Pond; and, the most convenient place for many loops, the Eagle Lake parking lot. To get to the Eagle Lake lot take ME 3 into Bar Harbor (instead of into the park), turn right at the junction with ME 233, head west, and reach the Eagle Lake lot on the right after 2.2 miles. NOTE: During the summer this lot fills up fast.

Sources of additional information:

Superintendent
Acadia National Park
Bar Harbor, Maine 04609

Bar Harbor Bicycle Shop
141 Cottage Street
Bar Harbor, Maine 04609
(207) 288-3886
This is an active mountain bike shop with rentals, information, and maps.

Acadia Bike Rentals
48 Cottage Street
Bar Harbor, Maine 04609
(207) 288-9605

Notes on the trail: This map shows 3 loops: Around Mountain (15 miles in length), Witch Hole Pond (6 miles), and Aunt Betty's Pond (6 miles). You can connect all three, plus many other loops. Some hints and tips on riding the trails:

a) All major intersections on the network are numbered and labeled with signs. Use these signs to decide which way to go. At some intersections, make sure you don't miss a third choice, which sometimes comes up after an initial two-way intersection.

b) Do the Around Mountain loop counterclockwise for the best views and descent.

c) Eagle Lake loop is well-worn and fairly crowded.

d) Day Mountain loop (bottom right corner, 5.5 miles), which also serves as a horse trail, is relatively sandy.

e) Watch out for hikers and horseback riders, especially when descending.

f) Do not ride on the single-track hiking trails.

RIDE 61 *UPPER RIDGE ROAD*

This 4.5-mile loop winds along a power line, through fields and meadows, and on a scenic rural road. There's some moderately challenging riding on single- and double-track trails through overgrown fields; you'll have to watch for the occasional hidden obstructions and mud holes. The ride begins along a power line for about a mile, then veers off. The last 1.5 miles is a scenic, paved rural road. In summer, wildflowers abound—Queen Anne's lace, clover, mustard grass—as well as birds, butterflies, and scenic views. On Upper Ridge Road there's a greenhouse that welcomes visitors.

General location: Four miles north of Waterville.

Elevation change: The terrain is relatively flat, but there are several short, steep ascents and descents on the power line and paved road.

Season: The best time to ride here is late June through the fall. Spring brings mud.

Services: Halfway along the ride there's food and drink at Irving's Truck Stop on ME 201. All other services are available in Waterville 4 miles to the south.

Hazards: Although power lines are popular mountain biking trails in many areas, some people wonder about traveling near electromagnetic fields and the

RIDE 61 *UPPER RIDGE ROAD*

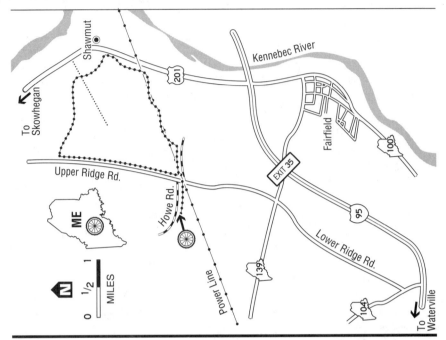

herbicides that may be used to clear undergrowth. This ride crisscrosses beneath high electricity wires for about a mile before veering off. To date there is no concrete evidence that either problem is worse than, say, visiting Boston for a day. And the scenery is much prettier. Watch out for some hidden ruts and obstructions in overgrown areas.

Rescue index: You are always close to civilization.

Land status: Private power lines and fields, with access informally given, and a state road.

Maps: USGS, Waterville, ME.

Finding the trail: Take Exit 35 on Interstate 95, heading north on ME 139 for three-tenths of a mile. Turn right on Upper Ridge Road, and reach the power line on the right after 1.1 miles. To park, turn left on Howe Road just after the trailhead and park at the bottom of the hill, before the road veers to the right.

Sources of additional information: C.M. Cycle in Waterville, (207) 873-5490, is a mountain biking shop.

Notes on the trail: The trail runs on the left side of the field, next to the tree line. But you first reach the trail by riding up a gravel road on the right side of the field and veering left, either across the field or just after passing a trailer home. The trail crisscrosses the power line several times. When you reach a fork on the right side of the line, turn left and cross underneath the line once more. You will come out in a clearing, with houses and a truck stop just beyond it. Fork right toward the truck stop. Ride into the parking lot behind the truck stop (on ME 201). There's a 24-hour convenience store and lots of big rigs here. Cruise around the parking lot and show off your rig.

Facing the field, fork right. Pass diagonally through the small field. If people are working there, indicate that you'd like to ride across it. Pick up the trail on the other side and go through an intersection of two trails. At a fenced-in field, turn left and pick up a smaller power line. About 1.2 miles from the truck stop, you will come out on Upper Ridge Road. Turn left and ride back on this rolling, scenic rural road.

RIDE 62 *WELD*

This easy 5.5-mile loop winds through lovely countryside, by a handsome farm, a river in the woods, and along fields with excellent views of 3,000'-plus mountains. After about two miles on two-wheel-drive roads you switch to a four-wheel-drive road for another two miles, and then return on one mile of pavement. The first stretch uses an authentic logging road (see "Logging Roads" below). There is also swimming at nearby Webb Lake and picnicking and nature hikes at Center Hill, located on the other side of Weld (see the Mt. Blue ride for directions to it).

General location: Town of Weld.
Elevation change: The ride begins at 690', ascends to 880', and descends on rolling terrain.
Season: Any time between mid-June and fall is fine for riding.
Services: All services are available in Weld. There is camping on Webb Lake in Mt. Blue State Park (for a fee).
Hazards: Watch for the occasional logging truck on the first leg of this ride. They're huge and they go fast. If you meet one, pull over and let it pass.
Rescue index: You are never far from civilization.
Land status: Town roads.
Maps: Any detailed state road map will do. Or pick up *The Maine Atlas and Gazetteer* (DeLorme Mapping Co., Freeport, ME), a collection of detailed road maps available in many stores.
Finding the trail: Take ME 142 north out of Weld (located 20 miles north of Rumford). After 2.2 miles turn left, following signs for Mt. Blue State Park and Webb Beach. After about a half mile park on the left side of the road, a few hundred feet before the road veers to the left at a large field.

RIDE 62 *WELD*

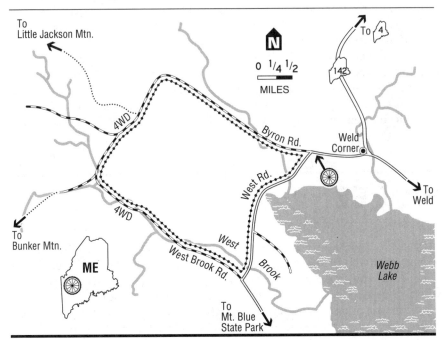

Sources of additional information:

Mount Blue State Park
Bureau of Parks and Recreation
(207) 585-2347

Notes on the trail: Ride up to the fork and go straight onto an unpaved gravel road. After 2.1 miles, turn left onto rougher West Brook Road. Veer to the left and ride along a brook. (To extend this ride, explore some of the trails branching off West Brook Road to the southwest.) After about 2 miles you will come out onto a paved road. Turn left and head back to the beginning of the ride. (There's a beach at Webb Lake about 6 miles to the right on this scenic paved road; but it's a steep climb to get there.)

NOTE: *Logging Roads.* Many unpaved roads in sparsely populated northern Maine are logging roads. These gravel "highways" are used almost exclusively by huge, fast-moving trucks. Some of the paper-producing companies who own these roads have banned biking on them for safety reasons. Others simply disapprove of biking. Some are trying to figure out ways to accommodate mountain biking (as well as other outdoor recreational sports) by, for instance, setting aside land for parks. If you want to ride on these smooth, endless dirt roads, first find out whose road it is. Ask in nearby towns, then call the appropriate paper company and query them on their logging road policy.

RIDE 63 MOUNT BLUE STATE PARK

You will ride through a secluded hardwood forest of maple, beech, ash, and birch on this moderate five-mile loop in a large state park. Along mostly rugged double-track trails you cross a stream or two, and you might even see a moose if you're quiet. For an easier ride, cruise along the smooth dirt Mt. Blue Road.

The ride runs along the western base of Mt. Blue. You can hike to its panoramic summit (3,000') from the parking lot. There's also swimming and camping at Webb Lake in the park, and picnicking and nature hikes at nearby Center Hill.

General location: Just north of Weld, and 20 miles north of Rumford, at the junction of ME 142 and ME 156.

Elevation change: The ride begins at 1,365', climbs steadily and gradually to 1,650', and descends more rapidly.

Season: There's plenty of mud in spring, making this ride best in summer and fall.

Services: All services are available in Weld, Mexico, and Rumford. There is camping at Webb Lake (for a fee).

Hazards: At the end of the ride there's a fairly steep descent on an old logging road with loose rocks.

Rescue index: You will be about 2 miles from an access road at the farthest. State Police Emergency Assistance: (800) 452-4664.

Land status: Old roads and state park trails.

Maps: USGS, Mt. Blue, ME.

Finding the trail: From ME 2, take ME 142, reaching Weld at the junction of ME 142 and ME 156. Keep going straight on Center Hill Road north of Weld. Veer left on pavement at a fork, following signs for Center Hill and the Mt. Blue Trail. You will pass a panoramic view on a hill on the left, and the state park headquarters building on the right. Keep going straight toward the Mt. Blue Trail at a left fork, and reach the parking lot after another 2.5 miles.

Sources of additional information:

Mount Blue State Park
Bureau of Parks and Recreation
(207) 585-2347

Notes on the trail: Ride back down Mt. Blue Road from the parking lot, until you reach a trail on the right after six-tenths of a mile. Ride up the trail for 1.4

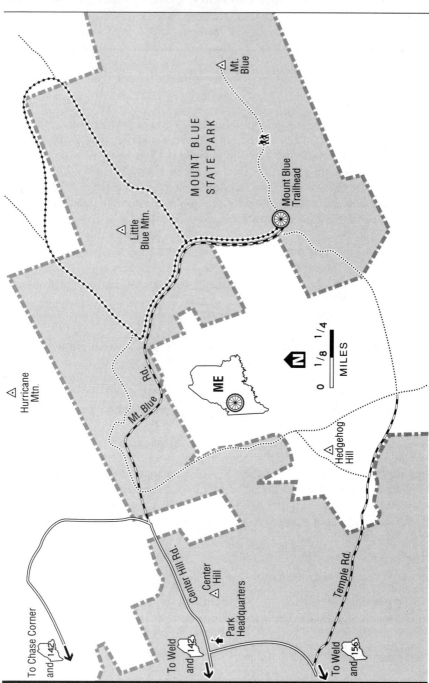

Mt. Blue

MOUNT BLUE STATE PARK

Mount Blue Trailhead

Little Blue Mtn.

Hurricane Mtn.

Mt. Blue Rd.

ME

0 1/8 1/4
MILES

Hedgehog Hill

Center Hill Rd.

Center Hill

Park Headquarters

Temple Rd.

To Chase Corner and 142

To Weld and 142

To Weld and 156

miles, until you reach a left turn with signs pointing all-terrain vehicles (ATVs) to the left. (The trail straight ahead is rideable, but it is hard to loop back from it.) After another mile you reach a "T" junction. Turn left and go downhill for seven-tenths of a mile. You will come out on Mt. Blue Road again. Turn left.

NOTE: *Snowmobile Trails.* During the winter, hundreds of miles of snowmobile trails appear in Vermont, New Hampshire, and Maine. All 3 states have active snowmobiling organizations that obtain permission from landowners to build and maintain extensive systems of trails. Often you can recognize these trails by their bright markers, which indicate turns, off-limits trails, and the direction of a nearby numbered highway. Some snowmobile trails aren't open for mountain biking in spring through fall. It is often hard to tell. For instance, "No Trespassing" signs may refer only to hunters and fishermen, or might mean the owners wish their land to be ridden only when it's frozen. Ask local mountain bikers, and *always* be considerate. For more information about snowmobile trails in Maine, write to: Maine All-Terrain-Vehicle Program, State House, Station #22, Augusta, ME, 04333.

RIDE 64 *BANGOR LINEAR PARK*

This eight-mile (round-trip) out-and-back ride is made up of three distinct parts: 1.2 miles on a smooth, urban cinder path; a mile on an overgrown, grassy single-track trail; and two miles on a funky jeep trail (with some mud holes and an occasional abandoned car or soda can). The jeep trail is also used occasionally by motorized dirt bikes.

This ride follows the lively Kenduskeag Stream (actually a river) from its mouth in Bangor through suburbs on a grassy shoreline, and then into light woods. Along the way, you ride through an active park and past a wooden observation deck over the river, where you can peer down into a holding pool of resting salmon.

General location: City of Bangor.
Elevation change: Flat.
Season: Any time between mid-June and fall is good for riding.
Services: All services are available in Bangor and Brewer. For two-wheeled needs try Pat's Bike Shop at 373 Wilson Street in Brewer, (207) 989-2900.
Hazards: Watch for pedestrians on the first section of this ride. On the second section, prickly overgrown raspberry shoots might be jutting out over the trail.
Rescue index: You are never very far from assistance on this ride.
Land status: This ride crosses a public park, private land with informal public access along the river, and an abandoned public road.

RIDE 64 *BANGOR LINEAR PARK*

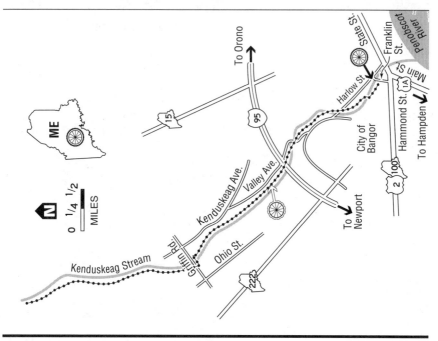

Maps: A map of Bangor will do.

Finding the trail: You can begin riding from either Franklin Street in Bangor or from a parking lot on the right side of Valley Avenue a few blocks north of US 2 and ME 100. If you begin on Franklin Street, pick up the gravel path on the northwest side of the bridge. To reach the parking lot on Valley Avenue from the south take US 1A Business into Bangor, and veer left onto Harlow Street, which becomes Valley Avenue.

Sources of additional information: Bangor Recreation Department, (207) 947-1018.

Notes on the trail: Head northward on the path, reaching a bridge (about a half mile past the parking area on Franklin Street). Get on the bridge and pick up the path on the same side of the river. (The trail on the other side becomes overgrown.) The path widens as it goes through a narrow, well-used park. At the end of the park, keep going straight along the shoreline on an informal single-track trail that is also used by fishermen. After about a half mile, fork right onto a dirt road that climbs to Ohio Street. Turn left across a new bridge (rebuilt in 1990) and pick up the trail on the other side of the river, still heading north. After about a half mile fork right toward the river, then fork right again in another half mile. Next, take a left, passing a pillbox-shaped building on the right and a clearing at the end of the road. Turn around here and retrace the route.

RIDE 65 *UNIVERSITY OF MAINE FOREST*

You can ride for about ten miles on trails and an old dirt road in this popular mountain biking spot next to the university. Although the terrain is flat, some of the trails are challenging because of protruding roots, as well as some mud, rocks, and loose sand. To maintain these popular trails, walk around or ride through mud holes, but don't ride around them. The forest is surrounded by cultivated fields, a cluster of dairy barns, paved roads, and university playing fields. One trail passes through a cornfield. Also, local riders put on an annual mountain bike race here.

General location: City of Orono.
Elevation change: The terrain is relatively flat with short climbs and descents.
Season: Any time from June through winter is fine for riding. These are popular cross-country ski trails, so avoid crossing ski tracks in the winter.
Services: There is water and a restroom in the university athletic building. All other services are available in Orono.
Hazards: Watch for joggers, who also use these trails.
Rescue index: You will be about a half mile from roads and homes.
Land status: University trails open to the general public.
Maps: Pick up a trail map at the Recreational Sports Office in the Memorial Gym (the large building with a giant "M" on it), next to the main parking lot. The office is open 7 days a week, year-round.
Finding the trail: From the south, take Exit 51 on Interstate 95. Veer right toward Orono, following signs to the right for the University of Maine. The campus comes up on the left after about a mile on College Avenue. Park in the university's large parking lot.

Sources of additional information:

Recreational Sports Office
University of Maine, Orono
(207) 581-1081

Notes on the trail: The forest lies just behind the campus. Ride past the tennis courts and playing fields and onto a paved bike path. A trailhead into the woods comes up on the right, opposite a cluster of fitness equipment. Some of the trails cross private land briefly, so be sure to stay on them. And don't startle joggers.

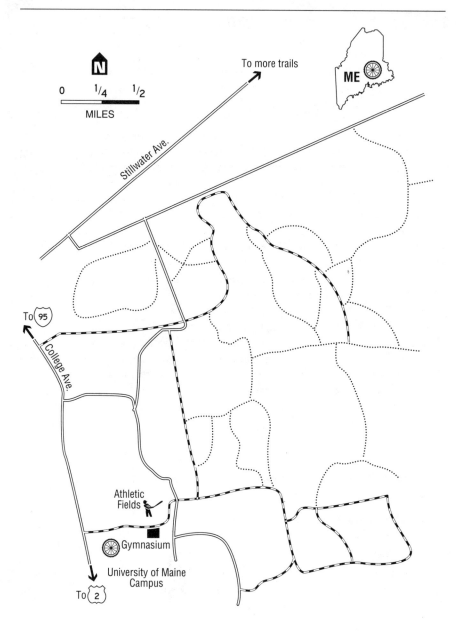

Note: *Ride is any trail or dirt road in the area.*

RIDE 66 *WIRE BRIDGE*

This moderately challenging 15-mile loop rolls along scenic two-wheel-drive dirt roads for about ten miles, then a wooded double-track trail for four miles, and finally a rural highway for a mile. First, you pass handsome farms and open fields. After this warm-up, the ride passes by a small airport in a field and heads into secluded woods on a jeep road that turns into a trail.

Along the first section of the ride there's a fun side trip to an unusual architectural structure—a 145-year-old suspension bridge made out of wire cables, wooden slats, and shingled towers. It is called (not surprisingly) Wire Bridge. There's also a local swimming hole at this unique bridge spanning the Carrabassett River.

General location: Just south of Kingfield on ME 16.
Elevation change: This is rolling terrain with regular, not-too-steep climbs on dirt roads and trails.
Season: Any time between late June and fall is good for riding. Snowmobilers pack down the trails during winter.
Services: All services are available in Kingfield.
Hazards: Watch out for occasional obstructions on the trail (ruts, logs, rocks) that can be obscured by vegetation in late summer. There is some traffic on ME 16 for the last 1.5 miles.
Rescue index: You are about 1 mile from assistance at the farthest.
Land status: Active town roads and abandoned county roads. Note: This ride closely passes several secluded homes. Be considerate and friendly.
Maps: USGS, New Portland, ME. Also, *The Maine Atlas and Gazetteer* (DeLorme Mapping Co., Freeport, ME), a collection of detailed maps, is available in many stores.
Finding the trail: From the south on ME 16, take a sharp left turn just before crossing the bridge into Kingfield, at a large barn on the left. From the north, the turnoff is a half mile east of the junction of ME 16 and ME 27 in Kingfield. Head south on Middle Road for a mile, until it becomes gravel. Park on either side.

Sources of additional information:

Holden Cyclery
317 Madison Avenue
Skowhegan, Maine 04976
(207) 474-3732
This shop can give you information about other rides in this area.

Notes on the trail: Head south on Middle Road for about 4.5 miles. To do a scenic side trip, turn right after 5 miles onto Wire Bridge Road. (A sign at the

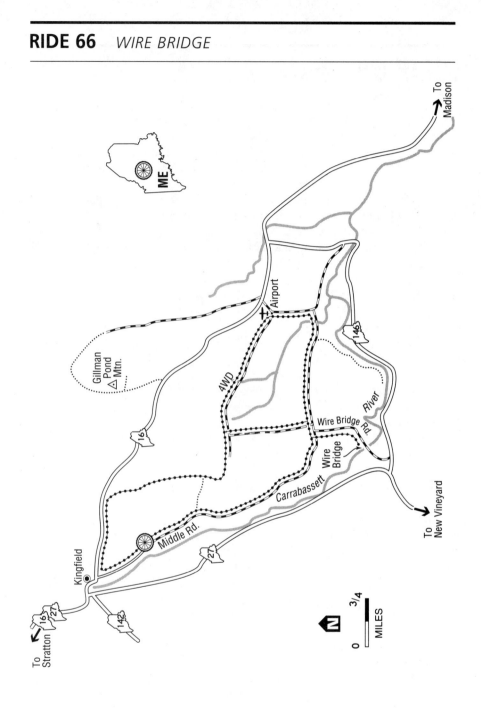

Grass-covered trail in late summer. Kingfield, Maine.

junction reads: "One Lane Bridge.") After 1 mile, you reach the historic bridge and swimming hole. Return to Middle Road, turn right, and ride for another 2 miles. (To do a shorter loop, just after Wire Bridge Road on the right, turn left onto another dirt road that climbs. At a "T" junction turn left onto the four-wheel-drive road that becomes a trail.) Turn left onto Millay Hill Road just after a brick house on the left. After about a mile, you will reach a fork at an island. Turn left and pass a private airport on the right. The road becomes four-wheel-drive, passes a junction on the left (the shortcut from Middle Road), and becomes a trail. The trail veers to the right and, after about 2 miles, while going downhill, forks left and comes out on ME 16. Turn left and ride on the gravel shoulder for 1.4 miles, until you reach the left turn onto Middle Road. Or veer right across a bridge and visit attractive Kingfield.

RIDE 67 *SOLON-BINGHAM RAIL TRAIL*

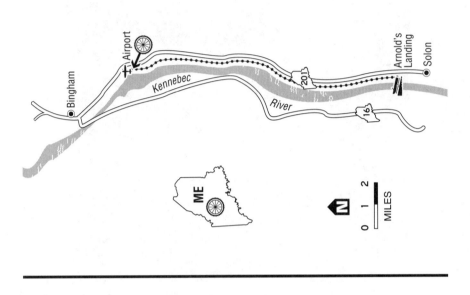

RIDE 67 *SOLON-BINGHAM RAIL TRAIL*

This 14-mile (round-trip) out-and-back ride follows a former railroad bed along the grand, wide Kennebec River. It's a breezy ride along fields, through occasional woods, and by commercial buildings. The trail itself is a narrow double-track path of packed sand and gravel. Like almost all rail trails, it's perfectly flat. There is a popular swimming spot and scenic falls at Wyman Lake, two miles north of the ride on ME 201. By the way, Bingham is exactly halfway between the North Pole and the Equator.

General location: Through the towns of Solon and Bingham, 15 miles north of Skowhegan.
Elevation change: Flat.
Season: This ride can be done in all 4 seasons.
Services: All services are available in Bingham or Skowhegan (10 miles south of Solon).
Hazards: None.

Rescue index: You are always close to roads and homes.

Land status: This former railroad right-of-way is now a public trail.

Maps: Any detailed state road map will show the location of the trail's endpoints.

Finding the trail: From the south on ME 201, turn left at the northern edge of Solon and follow signs to Williams Boat Launch Area on the right. There is plenty of parking at the launching area, which is next to the trail. From the north, go south from Bingham on ME 201 for a mile, then turn right into a large parking lot next to an airport and the White Water Information and Restaurant. (White-water sports are *big* in this region.)

Sources of additional information:

Holden Cyclery
317 Madison Avenue
Skowhegan, Maine 04976
(207) 474-3732

The Rails-to-Trails Conservancy
1400 16th Street, NW
Washington, D.C. 20036
(202) 797-5400

Notes on the trail: You can make this one-way ride into a loop by returning on US 201, which also parallels the river. It's a scenic highway with a reasonable bike lane.

RIDE 68   *CARRIAGE TRAIL / BIGELOW LODGE*

Climb to a large, secluded lake on this 10-mile out-and-back ride—20 miles round-trip if you continue to Bigelow Lodge on the lake. This ride is a steady, moderately difficult climb on a snowmobile trail. You pass through lush woods near a stream, cross feeder streams, and after about two miles, reach a side trail to Poplar Stream Falls on the right.

If you continue on a logging road for another five miles to Bigelow Lodge you will reach views of giant Flagstaff Lake and the surrounding mountains. The lodge is all that remains of a projected ski resort, meant to compete with nearby Sugarloaf USA, but never built. Today, the lodge is run by the state of Maine, which open it on weekends during the winter for snowmobilers. Depending on demand, it may soon be open during other seasons.

General location: Town of Carrabassett Valley (known locally as "Valley Crossing"), 12 miles southeast of Stratton on ME 27/16.

RIDE 68 *CARRIAGE TRAIL / BIGELOW LODGE*

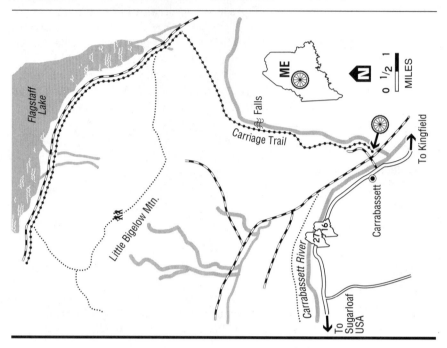

Elevation change: You begin riding at 850' and climb for about 2.5 miles to 1,100', for a total gain of about 250'. Then it's relatively flat.

Season: Any time between early June and winter is good for riding. The trail is fairly well drained in spring.

Services: Water is available at a spigot at the Carrabassett Valley town hall. There are well-stocked country stores on ME 27, and places to camp along the Appalachian Trail (which crosses the ride at about mile 12). For biking needs check out the bike shop at Sugarloaf USA (see "Sources of additional information").

Hazards: Watch for loose rock on the trail and an occasional vehicle on the logging road.

Rescue index: You are about 5 miles from traveled roads at the farthest. A rescue squad can be reached at (207) 237-3200 and is located in Carrabassett Valley near the trailhead.

Land status: An old town road and a logging road maintained by a snowmobile club.

Maps: *The Maine Atlas and Gazetteer* (DeLorme Mapping Co., Freeport, ME), a collection of detailed non-topographical maps, is available at many stores.

Finding the trail: The trailhead is 12 miles south of Stratton on ME 27/ME16. If you are coming from the south, turn right at a small sign for the Carrabassett

A friendly sign. Bigelow, Maine.

Valley Town Office, just after a tennis court with a housing development behind it on the right. If you see the Sugarloaf USA information building on the right on ME 27, you've passed the turnoff by about a half mile. Turn right and cross a bridge. Park in the town office parking lot on the left.

Sources of additional information:

> Sugarloaf USA
> Box 2287
> Kingfield, Maine 04947
> (207) 237-2000
> This large ski resort rents mountain bikes, gives lessons, and allows biking on its cross-country and alpine ski trails.

Notes on the trail: The trail up to the lake is easy to follow. After about 5 miles when you reach the dirt road at the southern end of the lake, you can take a side trip to the dam on the right, or turn left toward Bigelow Lodge. After about 5 miles on the road, you reach a large metal gate. The lodge is to the left at a fork. If you take the right fork you will reach the lake. Contact Blackwater Bikes in Davis for updated information about access to this area.

RIDE 69 *CARRABASSETT RIVER TRAIL*

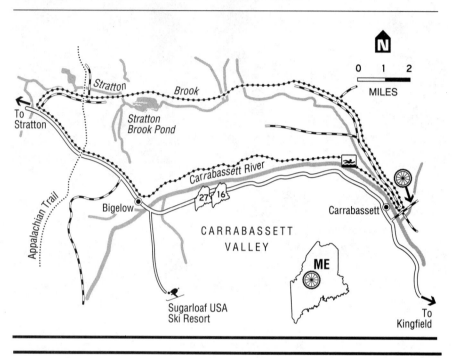

RIDE 69 *CARRABASSETT RIVER TRAIL*

RIDE 69 CARRABASSETT RIVER TRAIL

Mountain biking doesn't get much better than this 19-mile loop along a river and through pine-filled woods. (The first six miles can be done as a 12-mile out-and-back ride.) Along the dramatic Carrabassett River you maneuver on a narrow-gauge trail next to clean, clear water cascading over bedrock, where sun-bathers and swimmers relax in the summer. This popular trail joins a three-mile stretch on a scenic highway with unobstructed views of 3,000'-plus mountain peaks. Then you'll head into sweet-smelling woods, past a secluded lake and clearing with more good views.

Most of the ride is flat, with some technical riding on trails and one moderately steep climb on pavement. About 12 miles of the ride uses double- and single-track trails, livened up with a few mud holes and minor obstructions, four miles on jeep roads, and three miles on pavement.

General location: On ME 27, between Carrabassett Valley and Bigelow, 12 miles southeast of Stratton.

Log-jumping made easier. Carrabassett River Trail, Bigelow, Maine.

Elevation change: The first 6 miles of this ride follow a flat, abandoned railroad bed, followed by a short, fairly steep climb and a 2-mile descent on pavement. Finally, there are 9 miles of rolling terrain, climbing about 300', and then descending gently for 2 miles.

Season: Riding is good anytime between about mid-June and winter. There is mud in the spring; the first 6 miles are a popular cross-country ski trail.

Services: There are well-stocked country stores on ME 27 in Carrabassett Valley and to the north in Stratton. Water is available at a spigot at the Carrabassett Valley Town Hall (a trailhead). Camping is allowed along the Appalachian Trail, which intersects the ride on its second half. For biking needs, there's a shop at Sugarloaf USA (see "Sources of additional information").

Hazards: The highway has some traffic on it, but also a wide and well-paved shoulder. On the trail along the river watch out for hikers and bathers, especially around swimming holes.

Rescue index: You will be about 3 miles from traveled roads at the farthest. A rescue sqaud is located in Carrabassett Valley and can be reached at (207) 237-3200.

Land status: An old town road and abandoned railroad bed.

Maps: *The Maine Atlas and Gazetteer* (DeLorme Mapping Co., Freeport, ME) is a collection of detailed non-topographical maps, available in many stores.

Finding the trail: The trailhead is located 12 miles south of Stratton on ME 27/ ME 16. If you're coming from the south, turn right at a modest sign for the Carrabassett Valley Town Office, just after a tennis court with a housing development behind it on the right. (This junction is known as "Valley Crossing.") If you see the Sugarloaf USA information building on the right, you've passed the turnoff by about a half mile. At the sign turn left, cross a bridge, go up the road, and turn left on Huston Brook Road. After passing several summer homes, park off the road. You can also park in the town office parking lot just off ME 27 on the left.

Sources of additional information:

Sugarloaf USA
Box 2287
Kingfield, Maine 04947
(207) 237-2000
This large ski resort rents mountain bikes, gives lessons, and allows biking on its cross-country and alpine ski trails.

Notes on the trail: Ride up Huston Brook Road, which becomes four-wheel-drive, and at about 1.2 miles, fork left toward the river. The right fork is the road you'll be on at ride's end—although you can do this ride in either direction. The river trail, which becomes single-track, is easy to follow. After about 5.5 miles you pass several inhabited and abandoned buildings, the remains of the Bigelow Railroad Station. Turn right on ME 27, climb for a mile, and descend for 2 miles.

Turn right sharply onto a gravel road about 200 yards before a bridge on ME 27. It becomes a trail known as the old Stratton Brook Pond Road. After about 1 mile you intersect the Appalachian Trail. After another mile you will come to scenic Stratton Brook Pond. Watch for a fork after about another mile. Take the left one. The right one is an old logging road that becomes overgrown and impassable. The trail becomes a four-wheel-drive road and descends to the river, just above the trailhead.

Glossary

This short list of terms does not contain all the words used by mountain bike enthusiasts when discussing their sport. But it should be sufficient as an introduction to the lingo you'll hear on the trails.

ATB   all-terrain bike; this, like "fat-tire bike," is another name for a mountain bike

ATV   all-terrain vehicle; this usually refers to the loud, fume-spewing three- or four-wheeled motorized vehicles you will not enjoy meeting on the trail—except of course if you crash and have to hitch a ride out on one

bladed   refers to a dirt road which has been smoothed out by the use of a wide blade on earth-moving equipment; "blading" gets rid of the teeth-chattering, much-cursed washboards found on so many dirt roads after heavy vehicle use

blaze   a mark on a tree made by chipping away a piece of the bark, usually done to designate a trail; such trails are sometimes described as "blazed"

BLM   Bureau of Land Management, an agency of the federal government

buffed   used to describe a very smooth trail

catching air   taking a jump in such a way that both wheels of the bike are off the ground at the same time

clean   while this can be used to describe what you and your bike *won't* be after following many trails, the term is most often used as a verb to denote the action of pedaling a tough section of trail successfully

deadfall   a tangled mass of fallen trees or branches

diversion ditch a usually narrow, shallow ditch dug across or around a trail; funneling the water in this manner keeps it from destroying the trail

double-track the dual tracks made by a jeep or other vehicle, with grass or weeds or rocks between; the mountain biker can therefore ride in either of the tracks, but will of course find that whichever is chosen, no matter how many times he or she

	changes back and forth, the other track will appear to offer smoother travel
dugway	a steep, unpaved, switchbacked descent
feathering	using a light touch on the brake lever, hitting it lightly many times rather than very hard or locking the brake
four-wheel-drive	this refers to any vehicle with drive-wheel capability on all four wheels (a jeep, for instance, as compared with a two-wheel-drive passenger car), or to a rough road or trail which requires four-wheel-drive capability (or a *one*-wheel-drive mountain bike!) to traverse it
game trail	the usually narrow trail made by deer, elk, or other game
gated	everyone knows what a gate is, and how many variations exist upon this theme; well, if a trail is described as "gated" it simply has a gate across it; don't forget that the rule is if you find a gate closed, close it behind you; if you find one open, leave it that way
Giardia	shorthand for *Giardia lamblia,* and known as the "backpacker's bane" until we mountain bikers appropriated it; this is a waterborne parasite that begins its life cycle when swallowed, and one to four weeks later has its host (you) bloated, vomiting, shivering with chills and living in the bathroom; the disease can be avoided by "treating" (purifying) the water you acquire along the trail (see "Hitting the Trail")
gnarly	a term thankfully used less and less these days, it refers to tough trails
hammer	to ride very hard
hardpack	used to describe a trail in which the dirt surface is packed down hard; such trails make for good and fast riding, and very painful landings; bikers most often use "hardpack" as both a noun and adjective, and "hard-packed" as an adjective only (the grammar lesson will help you when diagramming sentences in camp)
jeep road, jeep trail	a rough road or trail which requires four-wheel-drive capability (or a horse or mountain bike) to traverse it
kamikaze	while this once referred primarily to those Japanese fliers who quaffed a glass of sake, then flew off as human bombs in suicide missions against U.S. naval vessels, it has more

recently been applied to the idiot mountain bikers who, far less honorably, scream down hiking trails, endangering the physical and mental safety of the walking, biking, and equestrian traffic they meet; deck guns were necessary to stop the Japanese kamikaze pilots, but a bike pump or walking staff in the spokes is sufficient for the current-day kamikazes who threaten to get us all kicked off the trails

multi-purpose   a BLM designation of land which is open to multi-purpose use; mountain biking is allowed

out-and-back   a ride in which you will return on the same trail you pedaled out; while this might sound far more boring than a loop route, many trails look very different when pedaled in the opposite direction

portage   to carry your bike on your person

quads   bikers use this term to refer both to the extensor muscle in the front of the thigh (which is separated into four parts), and to USGS maps; the expression "Nice quads!" refers always to the former, however, except in those instances when the speaker is an engineer

runoff   rainwater or snowmelt

signed   a signed trail is denoted by signs in place of blazes

single-track   a single track through grass or brush or over rocky terrain, often created by deer, elk, or backpackers; single-track riding is some of the best fun around

slickrock   the rock-hard, compacted sandstone which is *great* to ride and even prettier to look at; you'll appreciate it more if you think of it as a petrified sand dune or seabed, and if the rider before you hasn't left tire marks (through unnecessary skidding) or granola bar wrappers behind

snowmelt   runoff produced by the melting of snow

snowpack   unmelted snow accumulated over weeks or months of winter, or over years in high-mountain terrain

spur   a road or trail which intersects the main trail you're following

technical   terrain that is difficult to ride due not to its grade (steepness) but because of obstacles—rocks, logs, ledges, loose soil . . .

topo	short for topographical map, the kind that shows both linear distance *and* elevation gain and loss; "topo" is pronounced with both vowels long
trashed	a trail which has been destroyed (same term used no matter what has destroyed it . . . cattle, horses, or even mountain bikers riding when the ground was too wet)
two-wheel-drive	this refers to any vehicle with drive-wheel capability on only two wheels (a passenger car, for instance, compared to a jeep), or to an easy road or trail which a two-wheel-drive vehicle could traverse
water bar	earth, rock, or wooden structure which funnels water off trails
washboarded	a road with many ridges spaced closely together, like the ripples on a washboard; these make for very rough riding, and even worse driving in a car or jeep
wilderness area	land that is officially set aside by the Federal Government to remain *natural*—pure, pristine, and untrammeled by any vehicle, including mountain bikes; though mountain bikes had not been born in 1964 (when the United States Congress passed the Wilderness Act, establishing the National Wilderness Preservation system) they are considered a "form of mechanical transport" and are thereby excluded; in short, stay out
wind chill	a reference to the wind's cooling effect upon exposed flesh; for example, if the temperature is 10 degrees Fahrenheit and the wind is blowing at 20 miles per hour, the wind-chill effect (that is, the actual temperature to which your skin reacts) is *minus* 32 degrees; if you are riding in wet conditions things are even worse, for the wind-chill effect would then be *minus 74 degrees!*
windfall	anything (trees, limbs, brush, fellow bikers) blown down by the wind

PAUL ANGIOLILLO, a freelance writer and editor, has published many articles in *Bicycling*, the *Boston Globe*, *Business Week*, *Omni*, *Metrosports*, and *Dirt Rag*. Before mountain biking was born, he got his thrills dodging potholes in Boston, where he served as president of the Boston Area Bicycle Coalition. Today, he prefers tackling the dirt roads and overgrown trails surrounding a vacation home in New Hampshire. Paul lives in Waltham, Massachusetts.

The Mountain Bike Way to Knowledge is through William Nealy

No other great Zen master approaches William Nealy in style or originality. His handwritten text, signature cartoons, and off-beat sense of humor have made him a household name among bikers. His expertise, acquired through years of meditation (and some crash and burn), enables him to translate hard-learned reflexes and instinctive responses into his unique, easy-to-understand drawings. Anyone who wants to learn from the master (and even those who don't) will get a good laugh.

Mountain Bike!
A Manual of Beginning to Advanced Technique

The ultimate mountain bike book for the totally honed! Master the techniques of mountain biking and have a good laugh while logging miles with Nealy.

Soft cover, 172 pages, 7" by 10"
Cartoon illustrations
$12.95

The Mountain Bike Way of Knowledge

This is the first compendium of mountain bike "insider" knowledge ever published. Between the covers of this book are the secrets of wheelie turns, log jumps, bar hops, dog evasion techniques, and much more! Nealy shares his wisdom with beginner and expert alike in this self-help manual.

Soft cover, 128 pages, 8" by 5 1/2"
Cartoon illustrations
$6.95

From Menasha Ridge Press
1-800-247-9437

FALCONGUIDES   *Perfect for every outdoor adventure!*

Angler's Guide to Alaska
Angler's Guide to Florida
Angler's Guide to Montana
Backcountry Horseman's Guide to Washington
Birder's Guide to Montana
Birding Arizona
Birding Minnesota
Floater's Guide to Colorado
Floater's Guide to Missouri
Floater's Guide to Montana
Hiker's Guide to Alaska
Hiking Alberta
Hiker's Guide to Arizona
Hiking Arizona's Cactus Country
Hiking the Beartooths
Hiking Big Bend National Park
Hiking California
Hiking Carlsbad Caverns and Guadalupe National Park
Hiking Colorado
Hiker's Guide to Florida
Hiker's Guide to Georgia
Hiking Glacier/Waterton Lakes National Parks
Hiking Hot Springs in the Pacific Northwest
Hiker's Guide to Idaho
Hiking Maine
Hiking Michigan
Hiking Montana
Hiker's Guide to Montana's Continental Divide Trail
Hiker's Guide to Nevada
Hiking New Hampshire
Hiking New Mexico
Hiking North Carolina
Hiker's Guide to Oregon
Hiking Oregon's Eagle Cap Wilderness
Hiking Tennessee
Hiking Texas
Hiker's Guide to Utah
Hiking Virginia
Hiker's Guide to Washington
Hiker's Guide to Wyoming
Trail Guide to Bob Marshall Country
Trail Guide to Olympic National Park
Wild Montana
Rockhounding Arizona
Rockhound's Guide to California
Rockhound's Guide to Colorado
Rockhound's Guide to Montana
Rockhound's Guide to New Mexico
Rockhound's Guide to Texas

Rock Climbing Colorado
Rock Climber's Guide to Montana
Scenic Byways
Scenic Byways II
Back Country Byways
Scenic Driving Arizona
Scenic Driving California
Scenic Driving Colorado
Scenic Driving Georgia
Scenic Driving Montana
Scenic Driving New Mexico
Oregon Scenic Drives
Scenic Driving Texas
Traveler's Guide to the Lewis & Clark Trail
Traveler's Guide to the Oregon Trail
Traveler's Guide to the Pony Express Trail
Mountain Biking Arizona
Mountain Biker's Guide to Central Appalachia
Mountain Biker's Guide to Colorado
Mountain Biking the Great Lake States
Mountain Biking the Great Plains States
Mountain Biking the Midwest
Mountain Biker's Guide to the Ozarks
Mountain Biker's Guide to New Mexico
Mountain Biker's Guide to Northern California/Nevada
Mountain Biking Northern New England
Mountain Biker's Guide to the Northern Rockies
Mountain Biking the Pacific Northwest
Mountain Biking the Southeast
Mountain Biker's Guide to Southern California
Mountain Biker's Guide to Southern New England
Mountain Biker's Guide to the Southwest
Mountain Biking Texas and Oklahoma
Mountain Biker's Guide to Utah
Wild Country Companion

FALCON
1-800-582-2665

P.O. BOX 1718
HELENA, MT 59624

DENNIS COELLO'S AMERICA BY MOUNTAIN BIKE SERIES

Happy Trails

Hop on your mountain bike and let our guidebooks take you on America's classic trails and rides. These "where-to" books are published jointly by Falcon Press and Menasha Ridge Press and written by local biking experts. Twenty regional books will blanket the country when the series is complete.

Choose from an assortment of rides—easy rambles to all-day treks. Guides contain helpful trail and route descriptions, mountain bike shop listings, and interesting facts on area history. Each trail is described in terms of difficulty, scenery, condition, length, and elevation change. The guides also explain trail hazards, nearby services and ranger stations, how much water to bring, and what kind of gear to pack.

So before you hit the trail, grab one of our guidebooks to help make your outdoor adventures safe and memorable.

Call or write
Falcon Press or Menasha Ridge Press
Falcon Press
P.O. Box 1718, Helena, MT 59624
1-800-582-2665
Menasha Ridge Press
3169 Cahaba Heights Road, Birmingham, AL 35243
1-800-247-9437